MINDFULNESS
ON THE GO

MINDFULNESS ON THE GO

INNER PEACE IN YOUR POCKET

PADRAIG O'MORAIN

MINDFULNESS ON THE GO

ISBN-13: 978-0-373-89329-4

First published in Great Britain in 2014 by Yellow Kite,
an imprint of Hodder & Stoughton.
© 2014 by Padraig O'Morain

The health advice presented in this book is intended only as an informative resource guide to help you make informed decisions; it is not meant to replace the advice of a physician or to serve as a guide to self-treatment. Always seek competent medical help for any health condition or if there is any question about the appropriateness of a procedure or health recommendation.

Library of Congress Catalog-in-Publication data on file with the publisher.

www.Harlequin.com

Printed in U.S.A.

To Phil, Niamh, Hannah and Lil

HOW TO GET THE MOST FROM THIS BOOK

This book aims to give you an understanding of mindfulness with lots of ideas for how to practice it easily during your day. It is based on the author's 25 years of practicing and teaching, while also leading a busy family and work life.

You are welcome to read it straight through or to dip in at random—whichever you decide to do, it is important to read Chapter 1 first. While reading that chapter you will find yourself starting to be mindful without any effort, and by the end of the chapter you will have a good grounding in the subject.

Throughout the book I have included various **mindfulness exercises** which are spread throughout the text. These are signposted with an On the Go heading, so you can easily locate them. Each exercise offers a simple practice, designed to help you be more mindful during the day, with an option to go deeper and extend the practice should you wish.

Toward the end of the book there are two sections designed to help you make mindfulness part of your everyday life. The **Mindfulness Calendar** on p. 175 will help you remember to practice every day by inspiring you with ideas. Just find the day of the month and have a go at the suggestion for that date. The last section, **Ten Strategies for Everyday Mindfulness**, includes tips on finding windows of time for quick and effective mindfulness techniques.

At the end, the **Resources** suggest where to go for more ideas and guidance on mindfulness, including websites, books and apps.

Read the first chapter, read some more and then turn to the sections that you think might help you most. This book is a tool to be used, so make it work for you. Everything you need to practice mindfulness lies within these pages, so let's get started, and remember that practice is the key to developing this invaluable life skill.

CONTENTS

1

MINDFULNESS—AND WHY YOU SHOULD PRACTICE IT

Only a couple of decades ago few of us had heard of mindfulness, yet today it seems to be the word on everybody's lips, with big companies, sports organizations, hospitals, trade unions and all manner of individuals from tycoons to parents who are teaching or using it.

But one thing that puts many more people off trying out mindfulness is that they are convinced that it will take up more time than they can give to it. They know they are never going to sit and observe their breathing for twenty minutes a day. Indeed, you yourself may even have tried and given up when the busyness of life got in the way.

The good news is, however, that mindfulness is an attitude as well as a practice. And, even better, there are quite short practices that can help you to develop it and enjoy its benefits.

Even in this frantic world, mindfulness practice can give you a sense of spaciousness and a perspective that will help you to see more clearly what needs to be done at work, at home and at play.

So if you have very little time on your hands, but would like to give mindfulness a try, this book is for you. Let's begin with some of the reasons why you might *think* you can't practice mindfulness.

I CAN'T PRACTICE MINDFULNESS BECAUSE . . .

. . . I am too busy to be mindful. Awareness of what is going on right now in an accepting way—a key aspect of mindfulness—won't interfere with your busyness, but it will give you a welcome and valuable sense of calm and self-possession in the middle of it. For instance, glance around the space you're in right now. As you do so, can you put a very light attention on the sensation of your breath as it enters and leaves your nostrils? Let your mind go quiet for a few moments. That's a mindfulness practice, and it takes no more than a few seconds, yet it can help you to lift your head out of the busyness of your day.

. . . I am too busy to sit and meditate. As its title suggests, this book will show you how to practice mindfulness "on the go." None of the mindfulness practices in the book require you to sit and meditate for lengthy periods. For instance, breathing in to a count of seven and out to a count of eleven (the 7/11 practice—see p. 32) is very calming. It also takes less than half a minute to do. Try it and see.

. . . I'm a parent of young kids—where am I supposed to find quiet spaces in my life? That's OK: This book will show you how to practice mindfulness and scream at the kids at the same time! And if you learn to observe their shenanigans without crowding your mind with judgments about them—or about yourself—you might even scream less often. For instance, take a moment right now to notice where in your body you feel a sense of calmness and groundedness. This might be somewhere between your chest and your tummy or it might even be at the tip of your nose. Next time the kids are driving you mad (or you're driving them mad), try to retain an awareness of that center of groundedness.

. . . I can't do the lotus position and I don't like all this Buddhist stuff, anyway. Mindfulness has nothing to do with the lotus position. People who practice mindfulness in the Buddhist tradition sometimes meditate in that position, but I won't be asking you to do anything like that. Next time you're sitting in a chair, notice the feeling of your back against the back of the chair and of your feet against the soles of your shoes. That's a brief mindfulness practice that doesn't require the lotus position.

. . . I don't have the time to read long books about mindfulness. That's why, as books go, this is a short one. And it's designed so that you can dip in at any time to find a mindfulness idea or suggestion you can practice in a way that fits in with a busy lifestyle. For instance, what can you hear right now in your vicinity? Can you listen for about twenty seconds without telling yourself a story about the sounds and without interpreting them? As you do this, if a story or interpretation comes into your mind, return your attention gently to the sounds. That's an example of a mindfulness practice that you can do in a very short period of time (although, as with all the practices in this book, if you want to spend longer periods doing it or if you want to set aside a little time on the weekends for a mindfulness meditation, that's good too).

So now that we've dealt with potential obstacles and established that mindfulness might be for you, let's look at what it actually is and how it is good for you.

WHAT IS MINDFULNESS ANYWAY AND WHY WOULD I WANT TO DO IT?

Think of mindfulness as returning. It's as simple—and as difficult—as that. Mindfulness is about returning your attention again and again to whatever is going on for you right now—but in a special way: without arguing with reality (see "Mindfulness is acceptance"). By dropping that argument you learn to appreciate what is there to be appreciated and you enhance your ability to see what needs to be changed. The benefits are manifold, as I outline below.

Mindfulness is acceptance. I think this is probably the key thing to remember. Most of us find the concept of acceptance hard to understand. One of its meanings is that you don't use energy complaining to yourself about the things that you can do nothing about right now: it's raining outside or you don't like your job or your spouse is annoying. It is possible to waste vast amounts of energy complaining about things like these. But, ultimately, where does that get you? It doesn't stop the rain from falling, it won't make your job wonderfully exciting and it won't change your spouse's annoying habits.

We spend a lot of our time in a sort of trance, made up of memories, fantasies and other thoughts. This almost always holds us back. Instead, step out of the trance and into direct experience of your reality. If you practice mindfulness—by which I mean, among other things, stepping out of the old stories that your mind wants to tell you and learning to accept things for what they are—you may ruefully note these facts, but you will be less likely to argue with what you cannot change. You will also waste less energy getting stressed and upset about reality. And the extra energy—the extra mental space that you get from that—

will make you far more skilled at identifying what *is* in your control to do.

Try it now. If you have been complaining about something today, something that you cannot change, let the complaining fall away. Instead, put your attention on your breathing, your posture or your actions. Notice what you have just done: you have stepped out of your imaginary world and into the real world (through shifting your attention to breathing and posture). And by the way, that means you're already practicing mindfulness!

Mindfulness lowers stress and anxiety. What's the difference between stress and anxiety? Well, stress can be very short-term. If you're at a game and your side is tied with their opponents, that's stress. In a way, it's an enjoyable kind of stress, even if it doesn't feel like it at the time. But the game ends, your side has survived, lost or won the day with a last-gasp miracle, and then the stress is over.

Anxiety is different. Anxiety can gnaw away at you before the game begins, whether the "game" is a social or work situation or a game of football, and it can keep on gnawing afterward by transferring itself to the next game. Even the most avid fan is unlikely to stay awake at night worrying about those last three minutes of extra time. But he or she might stay awake indulging in anxiety about work, a relationship or health issue.

You will notice the benefits of mindfulness most clearly in relation to stress. Suppose you have five things that you must do and only enough time to do three of them. That, unfortunately, is the way we live today. If you become mindful, let's say, of your breath or your posture as you're working, you may begin to feel different, even though the demands on you have stayed the same. Mindfulness brings a sense of spaciousness, instead of that crowded feeling that can go with the state of being overwhelmed in which so many of us live now. Remember this: Stressing yourself out with negative scenarios will not alter the facts of what you have to do. Mindfulness, however, will help you to avoid adding more unnecessary stress. That, in turn, will benefit both your emotional and your physical health.

A mindful approach to anxiety would be to accept that anxiety comes into every life, even into every day and night. Be willing to experience such anxiety, as it is inevitable, but avoid exaggerating it with the stories you tell yourself about it. This storytelling is sometimes called "catastrophizing" and it can make anxiety far worse than it needs to be.

If you practice mindfulness by making it a part of your day, then your anxiety levels are likely to be far lower than if you had never done so. Mindfulness tends to calm, you could even say *cool down*, that part of the brain that triggers fight-or-flight response (see p. 22) and so often exaggerates harmless situations.

Mindfulness means a better approach to handling anger and resentment. These emotions disrupt peace of mind in all of us from time to time, and while mindfulness won't guarantee that you never feel them again (that's impossible in a world in which we so often rub each other the wrong way), if you are mindful you will avoid exaggerating your negative emotions. That's very important, especially in relation to anger.

Here is an example of a mindful approach to emotions: When you feel angry move your attention from your thoughts to how the anger feels in your body. Angry thoughts amplify the emotion of anger. But the physical sensation of anger will die down, as do all physical sensations. So if you practice shifting your attention from your thoughts to what the anger feels like in your body, you give the physical sensation and the anger time to die down. This can bring a lot of peace of mind if you find that anger and resentment disrupt your life.

Mindfulness boosts creativity. Is mindfulness all about calming stress and emotions? Not at all. It can actually unleash your creativity. For instance, people who value creativity and who practice mindfulness find that their intuition seems to work better. With a clear mind, ideas and solutions seem to come more easily.

There's nothing magical or mystical about this. Your mind often actually comes up with answers, but all too often you cannot hear them because of the chatter going on in your head. To help you visualize this, imagine a small child who knows the answer to a problem that all the adults in the room are discussing in loud, overlapping voices. The child pipes up, but cannot be heard. If you practice mindfulness, the "adults" in your head will quiet down and you will hear what the child is trying to say. That's one of the ways in which mindfulness boosts your chances of coming up with solutions that work. (I will return to this idea in Chapter 10, "Mindfulness at Work," where I talk about mindful planning.)

Moreover, if you're mindful you're less likely to follow old patterns of thought without question. That's important in business, in the home and in all other areas of your life. Some learned habits, like how to ride a bicycle, are really helpful, but others become creativity killers. As you go through this book, you will find that the practice of mindfulness encourages you to step out of those old habitual patterns.

Mindfulness in sports. Sportsmen and women also value mindfulness. Returning your focus to what is happening in the here and now is not only a fundamental aspect of the practice of mindfulness, it is also a key contributor to success in sports: A golfer who spends the next five minutes complaining to herself about her bad swing five minutes ago won't get very far in the game; neither will one who spends his time on the course glorying and fantasizing about the victory he hopes to have achieved by the time the game is over. The game takes place in the now and nowhere else.

Mindfulness makes home life better. For many, the home is the busiest place in their lives. Getting back from a day's work to the demands of kids and partners and whoever else might be around can be pretty stressful. That's especially so if you don't get time to kick off your shoes and chill out for a while before you have to get moving again. Mindfulness can help you to stay out of old patterns of reaction when you're on home ground. As we'll see in Chapters 7 and 9, we often navigate through our homes and our relationships simply by resorting to established patterns or old habits that don't serve us very well. But practicing mindfulness enables us to see this happening and to do something about it.

Mindfulness lowers the risk of depression relapse. Depression is an increasingly common experience for many people today. Even if you're lucky enough never to have been depressed, you probably know people who have suffered from this often debilitating condition. Research shows that mindfulness is of great value to people who suffer from recurrent bouts of depression by helping to protect against relapse. You will find more on this in the chapter on mindfulness and emotional distress (see p. 159).

It will help if you remember all the benefits outlined above as you read through this book and as you bring mindfulness into your life. And there's no need to rush it. Mindfulness is a gentle practice, and although most of the people I teach it to do begin to experience some benefits right away, remember you are trying out a whole new way of engaging with the world. You should, therefore, allow time for the full effects to come through.

In summary: Mindfulness is the practice of returning your attention again and again to what is going on, even if you don't like it, rather than spending time and energy on a struggle with reality. Mindfulness does not change reality directly, but it does change your relationship with it. And in doing that, it changes everything.

MINDFUL MOVEMENT

Practice: Notice the actions of walking or the physical movements associated with cooking or other manual activities.

Commentary: The kinesthetic sense—or perception—of how our bodies are moving is often only in our awareness when we grow tired or if we're running, cycling or dancing. But the awareness of movement is a very old mindfulness practice and you can use this in any circumstances: at your desk, in your car, cycling, doing chores around the house and so on. It's a great way to bring yourself into mindfulness while going about the ordinary business of your daily life and without having to set aside any special time.

If you want to go deeper: Deliberately slow down your movements for a while as an awareness exercise. Slow them down to a moderate level if you're at work or otherwise among people—in other words, just don't rush your movements. Now put your attention on the sensation of movement.

WALK MINDFULLY

Practice: Walk for a while with awareness of the movements of your body, perhaps noticing the air against your hands or your feet against the ground. Bring your attention back to your walking when you become distracted.

Commentary: This is one of the oldest of all mindfulness practices. If you're agitated, mindful walking can be especially helpful and calming. But you don't have to be agitated to benefit from this practice. Use it at work, for instance, when walking from one office to another. Or walk up and down the stairs at home mindfully to gain some presence of mind in the domestic emotional swirl.

If you want to go deeper: Try walking slowly, in a straight line back and forth or in a circle. Bring your awareness to every step as you lift and set down your feet. Coordinate your walking with your breathing.

SLOW DOWN

Practice: Now and then today, slow down whatever you're doing and pay attention to your actions: drinking tea, entering a password, opening a door, for instance.

Commentary: This practice immediately takes you out of your head and into mindful awareness. Technology and the demands made by ourselves and others encourage us to rush ever faster. Slowing down to practice mindfulness is an act of self-assertion. It is saying I am not on this earth to keep up—my life means more than that. It is pausing, every now and then, to bring yourself into your own presence.

If you want to go deeper: Continue this slow activity for longer. See also if you can bring about a slight slowing down of activities you engage in when other people are present—so slight that they don't notice, but you do.

THE SCIENCE OF MINDFULNESS

The effects of mindfulness on the brain have been studied extensively in recent years by neuroscientists and, so far, they have confirmed what mindfulness practitioners have known all along—namely, that this is a practice with many benefits, and that these benefits are real.

Before going into more detail, it's worth noting that much of the research is based on studying the effects of just eight weeks of mindfulness training—typically, two hours a week with forty minutes of meditation every day. Does this mean that you, too, must meditate for forty minutes a day to get the benefits of mindfulness? Not at all. Doing short mindfulness practices during the day and making this part of your routine will bring you the benefits—and that is what this book aims to teach you.

The research suggests that mindfulness practice gradually brings about certain changes in how the brain works. This is actually what you might expect, in the same way that you would expect those parts of the brain of a footballer that are involved in playing the game to strengthen over time.

MINDFULNESS AND THE BRAIN

Although the important point here is simply that practicing mindfulness makes your life better, many people (including neuroscientists) feel their practice is improved and encouraged by knowledge of how the brain is involved. So here are the main aspects, so far as they are known at this stage, of how your brain interacts with your practice of mindfulness.

From wandering to direct experience. That your brain wanders should come as no surprise. Morning, noon and night your wandering brain leads you off into memories, fantasies and thoughts of all sorts. You even go around talking to yourself—perhaps you are one of those people who talks to themselves out loud.

But what you might not know is that wandering is the normal state of the brain; indeed, neuroscientists refer to it as the brain's "default mode." If you are sitting doing nothing—at a desk, on a train, on the beach—your brain will take off into the past, the future, what might have been, what she said, what he said and so on. That's why it's impossible to remain completely mindful for a long time. It's also why there's no point in criticizing yourself for "being a million miles away" or "having your head in the clouds"—it's normal.

The problem with all that is this: when your brain and your mind wander you can fall into brooding about the past, which can lead to depression; or into recycling worries about the future, which can elevate anxiety; or into getting lost in fantasies, instead of making things happen in the real world (fantasizing about speaking a foreign language fluently, for instance, instead of getting down to learning it). And it's very seductive because the wandering mind is usually telling you stories about that most interesting of subjects—yourself: what happened to you, what someone did to you, what you might do next and so on.

Research shows that people who practice mindfulness spend less time wandering and more time directly aware of what's going on around them—which is hardly surprising because switching from wandering to direct experience is the major way in which we practice mindfulness. And the wandering switches off the moment you focus your attention which, with mindfulness practice, you do more often.

But the wandering only switches off for a while. It is ready at all times to pull you away again, like an old sailor who, on the slightest pretext, will recount stories of his glory days at sea until you lead him back to the present. That's why you have to return your attention again and again to your breathing or to other experiences in the real world.

Thinking system. The most recently evolved part of the brain is the cerebral cortex, which is the surface we see when we look at a picture of the brain. A really important part of the cortex that increases its activity when you practice mindfulness is the prefrontal cortex, located behind your forehead. This is where you make plans, figure stuff out, arrive at decisions and check that what you're planning to do is socially acceptable.

Another thing that mindfulness does is to strengthen the influence of the prefrontal cortex on the emotional center (the limbic system), and this is one of the ways in which you can become less reactive and take a more balanced view. If the influence of the prefrontal cortex is weak, you may be more prone to being hijacked by emotions, including, in some cases, those that can lead to anxiety and depression. By expanding the influence of the prefrontal cortex in various ways over time, mindfulness can reduce that reactivity and that susceptibility to these conditions.

Empathy and connection. Mindfulness can also boost the activity of the insula, an area of the brain involved in feelings of empathy— that is, understanding how someone else feels and being able to see the world through someone else's eyes. This is a hugely important skill, both in our close human relationships and in the workplace. The insula also plays a role in feelings of love, which may explain why people who practice mindfulness feel a stronger sense of connection with, and warmth toward, others. The insula also links awareness of your emotional feelings with awareness of your physical sensations. This, in turn, should strengthen your feelings of "being alive." Greater activity in this really important brain structure also increases your self-awareness which can help you develop and maintain presence of mind in a very busy, social world.

Positive emotions. People who practice mindfulness for a period of time (as short as eight weeks in one study) experience an increase in the activity of the left side of the brain called the anterior cingulate cortex. Activation of this left side is linked to positive emotions and a positive attitude. Mindfulness practice generally enables people to feel better over time and the anterior cortical area plays a role in this. This effect also helps to account for the value of mindfulness in reducing the risk of relapse into depression.

Fight-or-flight. As human beings we are emotional creatures and the all-important emotional (or limbic) system is located below the cortex, more or less between your ears. A key structure in the emotional system is the amygdala, which is involved with fear and fight-or-flight and, as such, is a crucial part of our survival kit. Because information coming through our senses arrives at the amygdala first, it assesses whether a situation is dangerous before the thinking part of the brain even gets to be aware of it. So if you are in danger, the amygdala sends a warning to the hypothalamus, which instantly alerts your "fight, flee or freeze" defense system. In this way, the amygdala's rapid assessment of danger helps to keep you out of trouble.

However, the fact that information comes to the amygdala first means that our emotional center becomes activated before our thinking comes into play. This "warn first, think later" system probably evolved many thousands of years ago to help us survive and pass on our genes. Then—and today!—if you were walking through the jungle and you saw something with black and orange stripes lurking behind a bush, your amygdala would send you scampering up a tree, just in case what you had seen was a tiger: Better to be safe than sorry. However, while this makes for an impressive defense system, it can also sometimes be unhelpful: when the amygdala is over-vigilant, it can create unnecessary panics, fears and anxieties, rather like an oversensitive burglar alarm or a nervous sentry who interprets every shadow as the approach of an enemy. People who have had frightening experiences, for instance, can suffer in this way from an amygdala that has become too highly sensitized.

So it's helpful to know that mindfulness practitioners become less reactive in the emotional part of the brain—that is, the amygdala calms down. This doesn't turn you into a zombie, though. The insula, remember, helps you to feel more connected to other people and is strengthened by mindfulness practice. And there is no evidence to suggest that this calming down can make you fail to spot real danger. In essence, it's just that you gradually become better at choosing a response instead of reacting blindly, but when you are in real and immediate danger, the amygdala will still spring into action and do its job.

Shifting perspectives. Brain regions linked to switching our perspectives are enhanced by mindfulness practice. An example might be seeing a situation from another person's point of view (the development of the insula, mentioned above, is involved here). Another shift is seen in a growing capacity to return our attention to our breathing or elsewhere, so as not to become hijacked by emotional reactions. In other words, as you practice returning your awareness again and again to your breath or your body, you gradually train your attention and become able to focus it more quickly and for longer periods of time. This improvement in attention is linked to increased activity in the lateral prefrontal cortex and is seen in people who practice mindfulness.

So while with mindfulness you will find it easier to become aware of all the sounds and activities around you, if you need to shift attention on to something specific—such as the task at hand—then you can do that very effectively because of that increased capacity for paying attention.

Perception of pain. Mindfulness practice has been found to reduce the brain's perception of the intensity of pain and the emotional distress arising from it. This is the basis of the eight-week Mindfulness-Based Stress Reduction (MBSR) program, originally developed for people in chronic pain. It is also the basis of the Breathworks program. If you wish to use mindfulness in dealing with pain, you will probably find one or more of these courses in the vicinity or region in which you live. (See more on Breathworks in the Resources section on page 215.) From a mindfulness perspective, people with pain are encouraged to focus attention on the pain itself and not on the distressing thoughts and images arising from it. This removes a layer of distress, but the focus on pain also seems to reduce the brain's sensitivity to the experience of pain itself. Further research into this effect still needs to be done, but findings like these have led hospitals and pain clinics around the world to introduce mindfulness programs into their treatment plans. If you are especially interested in this aspect of mindfulness, the book *Mindfulness for Health* by Vidyamala Burch and Dr. Danny Penman is well worth reading.

HOW ARE THE EFFECTS OF MINDFULNESS RESEARCHED?

Much of the research into the effects of mindfulness is done through the use of MRI (Magnetic Resonance Imaging) and fMRI (the "f" is for "functional") scans. MRI scans show a picture of the structures of the brain at any one time; fMRI scans depict the flow of blood in the brain (as different regions of your brain become active, they require more energy and this is delivered by means of an increased bloodflow to that region). So doing math will activate one region of the brain, remembering the last time you were angry will activate another and so on.

A WORD OF CAUTION

It is easy to become fascinated by the research on mindfulness and the brain, but what matters most of all is that you practice mindfulness in your own life. However, knowing that these very real changes I have described have been found in the brains of mindfulness practitioners is an added incentive to do it. The benefits of mindfulness are not simply a matter of opinion—they are scientifically validated. So if you find mindfulness practice difficult or you struggle with it at times, remember that the rewards are real—they are not "all in the mind."

3

WHY YOUR BREATH IS
YOUR BEST MINDFULNESS TEACHER

Are you breathing? Are you sure? Good. Now read on...

TWENTY THOUSAND BREATHS:
YOUR EVER-PRESENT MINDFULNESS TOOL

Each of us takes about 20,000 breaths a day. We are entirely unaware of most of these, which is fine. What I want to highlight though is that the breath can be of enormous help in maintaining mindfulness and a state of calm and presence of mind. Remember, the route to success in mindfulness is returning your attention again and again to what is actually happening right now. Your breathing is happening right now. Every time you return your attention to your breathing, you build your "mindful-ness muscle."

I think you will like the various approaches to mindful breathing in this chapter. If, however, you are a person who feels panicky or nervous when you observe your breathing, skip this chapter and instead use mindfulness of the body, of walking or of sounds, as a way of getting into the mindfulness zone. (You will find ideas on how to do this in Chapter 4, Your Mindful Body.)

Finding the anchor point. We begin our exploration of mindfulness of breathing with one of the most useful mindfulness techniques you could hope to find. Indeed, if you only want to learn a single mindfulness-of-breathing approach this, in my opinion, is the one to choose.

For a few moments, as you breathe, identify where in your body you most notice your breath. You can think of this as a sort of "anchor point" to which you can return whenever you want to get into the mindfulness zone. This could be very useful, especially if you're in a setting in which you would like to regain your presence of mind, such as the boardroom, the kitchen or on the street. Go to that place in your body where you can feel yourself connecting most with your breath. That could be at the tip of your nose, inside your nostrils, your lips if you are breathing through your mouth, the back of your throat or your chest. When you have located that point, breathe in and out for a little while, noticing the sensation of the breath. Whenever you want to be mindful, immediately connect with the present moment by switching your attention to the anchor point. So at night, for example, when thoughts are racing around your mind and you would rather be asleep, bring your attention to the anchor point. This can take you straight out of those unhelpful thoughts and into awareness of your breath.

At any time, it can be very comforting to return to the anchor point and it's extremely simple to do once you have located it.

○ IN A NUTSHELL: Identify where you most notice your breathing (e.g., the tip of your nose) and bring your attention to that anchor point whenever you want to come into mindfulness.

7/11 breathing. This is one of the easiest mindful techniques available. It couldn't be simpler and yet it's a powerful little practice. To do it, you count silently to seven as you breathe in and then you count silently to eleven as you breathe out. Counting helps keep your mind on the simple act of breathing. The technique naturally brings about a longer out-breath (more about this below).

◯ IN A NUTSHELL: Take a couple of breaths during which you breathe in to a count of seven and out to a count of eleven.

Focus on the out-breath. What's special about the out-breath? The out-breath engages the parasympathetic nervous system, which helps calm you down. It can bring you a sense of presence of mind, even in quite tense situations: at home, in business, before or after playing sports, shopping and so on. When you want to gain presence of mind or a sense of calm, the out-breath can be your friend. Follow your out-breath all the way out—it will feel as though it is going through your body right down into the floor or the ground. Focus on the out-breath also for a little while if you're trying to sleep or rest.

◯ IN A NUTSHELL: Rest your attention on your out-breath, all the way out for a calming mindfulness practice.

Counting the breath. Another effective way to keep your attention on your breathing for a few minutes is to count each complete in- and out-breath. Silently count "one" after the first in-breath and out-breath, two after the next, three after the next and so on, up to seven. When you get to seven, return to one again. If your mind wanders and you get lost, return to one and start again. Why only count to seven before you return to one? It's so that you won't get into a competition with yourself to see how many breaths you can count. The practice is about awareness of breathing and not how many breaths you can take.

◯ IN A NUTSHELL: When you want to keep your attention on your breathing, count each complete in- and out-breath until you have counted seven cycles and then start again. In other words, "In-out one," "In-out two," and so on.

Breathing without over-managing. Our bodies are very good at breathing without any direction from us or from our minds. But, like bad managers, we find ourselves irresistibly drawn to interfering whenever we actually notice that we are breathing. Can you rest your attention on your breathing without trying to manage or meddle with the process? You may be surprised by how difficult, almost impossible, it is to breathe without interfering, but making the attempt is a great way to focus your attention. It's also relaxing and enjoyable. As you observe, your breathing will almost certainly become slow and gentle.

◯ IN A NUTSHELL: Try allowing your body to breathe without interfering or directing the process in any way.

Pause at the end of the out-breath. A great deal of mindfulness practice is about pausing. A pause takes you back to yourself, out of the rush of events and out of the endless stories your mind wants to tell you. A pause restores you to yourself. I'm sure that from time to time you have found yourself working frantically, at the mercy of deadlines. To pause mindfully, even for a few moments, can restore your presence of mind in these situations.

We often pause naturally at the end of the out-breath. You may never have noticed it; most people don't until they deliberately start paying attention to their breathing as it is very quick and subtle. If you really pay attention, though, you'll notice that pause. It's a very, very short pause.

When you're focusing on your breath, observing the pause helps you keep that focus. Moreover, the pause happens in the here and now and takes you straight into the present moment.

Don't try to manage the pause, though. Try to observe it as it occurs, for however brief a period that might be. Then allow the next breath to occur naturally, as soon as it wants to. It's like standing on a beach as the tide is beginning to come in. Slowly, the water comes to your feet, seems to pause and then ebbs away. Then another pause, and it comes in again.

When you're lying awake at night and would prefer to be asleep, putting your attention on your out-breath is really helpful, as I have recommended above, but include the pause at the end of the out-breath too. It will take your mind off whatever you might be worrying about and on to the simple act of breathing.

◯ IN A NUTSHELL: As a way of focusing your mind, notice the tiny pause at the end of your out-breath.

Is that a feather at the end of your nose? Here is a simple way to focus your attention on very gentle breathing: Imagine that a small feather is hovering at the end of your nostrils; try to breathe so gently that the feather doesn't move. You can even keep your eyes open if you want. Notice how you have to really focus attention on your breathing to make sure the feather doesn't move? Even a minute of this feather practice will bring your scattered mind right back into the moment. This is also a really good exercise if you want to relax. You can use the feather technique anywhere; after all, nobody can see the feather but you.

◯ IN A NUTSHELL: Imagine a little feather at the end of your nose. Try breathing so gently that it doesn't move.

Tummy, chest, back. You are familiar with the sensation of your rib cage expanding and contracting as you breathe. But if you pay attention, you'll notice that your back also widens and narrows as you breathe. Similarly, you are probably aware of the sensation of your tummy expanding and contracting as you breathe. But the lower back also contracts as you inhale and expands as you exhale. Sometimes the movement is very subtle, which makes it all the more helpful as a focus for attention.

You can also notice the feeling of your entire body breathing. Really, this is an extension of what I have talked about in the previous paragraph but, again, it focuses your attention on that wonderful sensation of breathing. It takes you straight back into the "now" where your breathing always resides. If it helps, imagine that inside your trunk (chest and tummy) there is a balloon of any color you like—even a multicolored one, if you prefer—and it is expanding and contracting as you breathe. (I suggest this as an exercise for small children in Chapter 7, Mindfulness at Home, but it can work for you too.)

The tummy-chest-back approach gets you out of your head and into your body. It's terribly easy to think that our whole world exists inside our minds—but it doesn't. When you calm the body, you calm the emotions. By focusing on the body as you breathe, you will discover a sense of peacefulness and well-being if you devote a little time to it.

○ IN A NUTSHELL: Notice how your tummy, chest and back move as you breathe.

Breathe in the negative. Finally, I want to share a different way of working with the breath. I have used this while walking, sitting on the train or at my desk, and in many other situations. It is an old Tibetan practice, but one that is still very useful today.

Imagine that you are breathing in your own emotional negativity and that you are breathing out peace. If you are not feeling negativity right now, you can simply imagine you are breathing in the world's pain and breathing out peace. Here are some examples (you can choose whichever is relevant to you at any given time):

- Breathing in fear. Breathing out peace.
- Breathing in frustration. Breathing out peace.

- Breathing in my family's (friends' or anyone else's) distress. Breathing out peace.

- Breathing in the overwhelming day. Breathing out peace.

- Breathing in loss. Breathing out peace.

What is unusual about this practice is that you breathe *in* the negativity instead of trying to expel it by breathing it out. This is entirely in line with mindfulness practice in which we experience and accept what is going on for us without denying reality. And in saying "Breathing out peace" you are not trying to get rid of it; instead, you are sharing it with the world or with whoever might be on your mind. In doing so, you gradually develop a sense of peace in yourself.

Try this at your desk, in traffic, at home or anywhere it might be helpful. Even at the start of a very demanding day you could spend a minute or so, perhaps, saying "Breathing in anxiety. Breathing out peace." Then return to it during the day. You don't have to sit down or close your eyes (though I find that to be a good way to start the day, for just a few minutes); the key is to step out of the story your mind wants to tell you about how awful things are and, instead, breathe in that "awfulness" and breathe out peace.

◯ IN A NUTSHELL: Sit for a minute or so and imagine you are breathing in your anxieties, fears, anger, etc., and breathing out peace.

In summary: Every time you check in with your breathing, you become mindful. Your breathing doesn't take place in the past, nor does it take place in the future; it takes place in the present moment. That's why mindfulness practitioners and meditators have used awareness of breathing for thousands of years as a way to anchor themselves in the present. Whichever of the practices in this chapter appeal to you the most, they are the ones you should use. Whenever you check in with your breathing, especially at the anchor point (see p. 30), you'll be practicing mindfulness. So go ahead—make your breath your best mindfulness friend.

ONE BREATH OUT,
ONE BREATH IN

Practice: Pause and follow your out-breath all the way out in awareness and then follow your in-breath all the way in.

Commentary: You can do this simple practice at your desk, working in the kitchen, stalled in traffic and in many other everyday situations. The out-breath is particularly calming and that is why I suggest you start with it. Even in the short time it takes to do this, your mind may drift. When you notice this, bring your attention back to your breath. Bringing your attention back again and again is the essence of mindfulness. Remember, if your mind didn't wander you couldn't bring it back—so no criticizing yourself for drifting.

If you want to go deeper: Take the time to notice the little gap at the end of the out-breath before you breathe in again. Allow the out-breath to occur naturally, without interference.

NOTICE THE PAUSE

Practice: Be still and notice the pause at the end of the out-breath, before the in-breath begins.

Commentary: The pause at the end of the out-breath is so short that to notice it you have to pay attention and come out of your thoughts. Becoming aware of the pause brings you into stillness, even if only for a little while. Even that short stillness can prevent you from being swept away by the flow of events. Don't try to lengthen the pause or to manage it in any way. Become aware of it, observe it and settle into its silence. Then observe it being replaced, quite naturally, by the in-breath.

If you want to go deeper: Observe the pause for a few breaths, noticing how your body and mind become still for that space of time. See if you can maintain that sense of stillness for at least part of the in-breath that follows the pause.

AN HOUR HAS PASSED

Practice: Whenever you notice an hour has passed, return your attention to your breathing for a few moments.

Commentary: Like many people, you may find it easy to be mindful at the start of the day. However, as the hours go by, the busyness of the day takes over and pushes mindfulness away. With that busyness can come unnecessary physical and mental stress. You face the world with shoulders raised, face frowning, mind preoccupied with the next thing and the next thing and the next thing. Loss of mindfulness can mean you put more stress into your activities than is needed and end the day feeling more tired than necessary. Returning to your breathing whenever you notice another hour has passed can help you avoid unnecessary stress.

If you want to go deeper: Notice the breath entering at your nostrils or lips. Follow it down to your tummy. Wait for the out-breath to happen and follow it. Notice any movements in your body as you do this.

THE ANCHOR POINT

Practice: Identify where in your body you feel most aware of your breathing. This is your anchor point. Return your attention to that anchor point whenever you want to come into awareness or presence of mind.

Commentary: Where do you feel most aware of your breathing? For some it's in the nostrils or at the tip of the nose, for others the lips. For yet others it's the back of the throat, the chest, tummy or diaphragm (between chest and tummy). If you sit still and observe your breathing for a minute or so, you will easily identify this point. Think of this as your anchor point, a point to which you can return when you are caught up in thoughts, emotions or activities. As time goes on and as you practice, the anchor point will become more effective as a means of entering mindfulness.

If you want to go deeper: Focus on the anchor point for a couple of minutes. Become aware of your posture as you do so. Notice your body breathing, but with the anchor point at the center of it. Every time your attention wanders return it gently to the anchor point.

7/11 BREATHING

Practice: Breathe in while you count to seven; breathe out while you count to eleven.

Commentary: You can use this popular, brief mindfulness practice anywhere: sitting at your desk, working in the kitchen, stalled in traffic, on the sports field and in many other situations. The counting helps you concentrate on your breath and generates a longer out-breath. This, in turn, is calming. As you are breathing, notice the movements of your body—your chest and tummy expanding and contracting and your back widening and narrowing, for instance.

If you want to go deeper: If you can get a couple of minutes to yourself before meetings or encounters, do 7/11 breathing for three in-breaths and three out-breaths. This will send you into the situation with a valuable presence of mind. If you have the opportunity, you might want to repeat this exercise after the meeting or encounter.

4

YOUR MINDFUL BODY

We live in the age of the downgraded body. In other words, we live to a far greater extent in our minds than in our bodies and, I suspect, to a far greater extent than did previous generations. This comes at a cost, though, for if we lose touch with our bodies, we lose touch with ourselves. Mindfulness reconnects us with the body—because, despite the "mind" in mindfulness, the practice engages far more with the body than with our thoughts.

Let's begin our exploration of mindfulness and the body with a look at the role of physical sensations in emotions.

PHYSICAL EMOTIONS

You might be thinking emotions are mainly in the mind. However, they are to a great degree physical: when you feel angry, you feel a physical sense of anger, perhaps a tightening of your chest; when you are sad, that sadness is all too obviously physical with tears or a lump in your throat. Even boredom can manifest as a sort of physical slackness.

In mindfulness, we pay less attention to the mind, and especially to our thoughts, and we pay more attention to what our senses bring us. And our senses, after all, are physical: We see, hear, feel and touch through our physical senses.

Here is an example of how we can use mindfulness of our senses to help us with our emotions. Let's suppose something happened in the past that made you angry, and that every time you think of it you get angry again. When you feel that anger at least two things are happening: you're having angry thoughts (possibly angry images or scenes passing before your eyes and angry dialogue) but you also feel physically tensed up, maybe even physically warmer.

In mindfulness, you would be encouraged to focus on those physical sensations of anger, instead of getting lost in the angry story in your mind. You might find it easier to connect with your physical anger by imagining it as an area in your body that's glowing red.

I probably don't have to tell you that an angry story can go on and on and on, getting endlessly worse and worse. You might know people for whom an angry story has gone on for years or even decades; sometimes we see people allowing their whole lives to be bound up in anger. That's an extreme example, but it can happen in small ways to all of us. In other words, that's what happens when we allow ourselves to get lost, again and again, in the stories our minds tell us.

So how can you avoid falling into this emotional quicksand? If you get caught in an angry story you can move your attention on to how you feel physically—the physical sensation of anger. That feeling may be hot or cold, tight or loose, large in area or small, still or pulsating. Most likely, if you observe for a while, you will notice these characteristics changing. Physical feelings have a beginning and end. So the physical feeling of anger will gradually die away. It may come back again, but it will die away again. Sometimes it dies away because something else takes your attention. Sometimes it dies away because that is what physical feelings do.

Try this the next time you feel angry: Pay attention to the physical feeling without following the stories your mind wants to tell you and see what a huge difference it can make. This can be especially helpful when you're angry about something that happened in the past and that you cannot fix. You can calm the physical sensation and make a difference to how you actually feel.

Those past events that you can do nothing about can often lead to resentment—something that mindfulness practice is very helpful in dealing with. As with anger, the first thing to do is transfer your attention away from thoughts concerning the cause of your resentment and on to the physical sensation of resentment.

○ IN A NUTSHELL: When you feel resentment, anger, sadness or other "negative" emotions, become aware of the physical sensations that go with them, instead of getting lost in your thoughts.

CALMING THE EMOTIONS

Calming the body calms the emotions. Indeed, some psychologists have long believed that our emotions begin with the physical sensation. In other words, we notice the sensation first and we then experience this as an emotion. Whether or not you agree with this, I think you will have found, at the very least, that emotions do have a strong physical element. And what that means is that if you can calm your physical body, then you can calm your emotions too. Therefore if you're upset, doing the body scan (see p. 54) or walking mindfully (see p. 53) will calm the emotion that is upsetting you.

Have you ever been in a swimming pool with a wave machine? Waves surge periodically through the pool, which is fine if that's what you want, but not if you wanted a quiet time in the water. Think of the waves as your emotions, and the thoughts and stories in your head as what make those emotional waves—when practicing mindfulness of the body we switch off the wave machine and allow the water to calm.

○ IN A NUTSHELL: Relaxing your body helps to calm your emotions.

POSTURE AND MINDFULNESS

Being mindful of your posture is about being aware of whatever posture you are using right now, whether that is walking, sitting, standing or lying down. I would especially recommend this practice to you if you are a person who is very impatient with the idea of sitting down and becoming aware of your breathing for a few minutes. Instead, try to maintain an awareness of posture as you go about your business. You will find that this practice will keep you grounded and in the moment and will bring you all the benefits of mindfulness. Like most mindfulness practices, this one is also very discreet. You can sit at your desk being mindful of your posture and nobody but you will be any the wiser. Simply notice the feel of your body from head to toe, including the shape of your spine, and maintain that awareness for a few moments. If it helps, notice how you are breathing at the same time.

◯ IN A NUTSHELL: Becoming aware of your posture, whatever it may be, provides a quick and effective way to come into the mindfulness zone.

MINDFUL WALKING

For a very long time, perhaps thousands of years, walking has been used as a mindfulness practice. To practice mindful walking, bring your attention to your feet as they touch the ground or to the movement of your arms as you walk along. You might look at whatever is moving in your field of vision, such as birds flying across the sky or leaves in the breeze. If you are walking beside water, you might practice awareness of waves, ripples or the movement of swimming birds. Sometimes this can feel like "switching on" a new reality, but it's one that is always there: You just don't notice it most of the time.

The key point here is that you are mindful of your walking as you walk. You may walk slowly or briskly, as you prefer. Research shows that people's moods improve after a brisk walk and that the improvement lasts for at least a couple of hours after they have stopped walking; however, many people prefer to walk slowly as a mindfulness practice. It is up to you, but either way the practice will help you feel better.

If you can walk in the park or in the field by a river or canal, all the better. Taking a walk in a green, natural space tends to be more calming than walking along the street, for example. But if you don't have the opportunity to walk among greenery, that doesn't mean you can't benefit from walking practice. Even walking on the street or around the block, but in a mindful way, is a form of mindfulness practice. Or you could walk around your garden or even inside your own home. I have sometimes walked back and forth mindfully from the front to the back of the house for twenty minutes as a practice. Needless to say, I do this when nobody is around to comment on what I'm doing! You can do the same.

○ IN A NUTSHELL: Walking with awareness of what you are doing is a good, traditional mindfulness practice, especially—though not only—if you feel agitated or impatient.

THE BODY SCAN

In many respects, the body scan is a gift that you give to yourself. For five to ten minutes, you stop rushing and racing, you stop putting your body through its paces and you simply allow yourself to be. Practices such as this can bring back that unhurried sense that was so familiar to people in many societies in the past and is a rarity today.

For people who think too much, the body scan can bring about a much-needed rebalancing, so you will find it particularly valuable if you are someone who spends an awful lot of time in their head. The body scan is also a great tool to help you sleep—or to get back to sleep—at night, especially if you take your time with it.

To do the body scan, lie or sit down and connect with the feeling of your body. In other words, allow your attention to rest on the different parts of your body, one by one, in sequence—from your toes, right up to the top of your head, going all the way up in stages. So you move from your toes to the rest of your feet, then on to your calves, knees, thighs, hips, back, chest, tummy, arms, hands and shoulders. Then scan the back of your neck, back of your head, forehead, eyes, jaw and face. The practice is no more complicated than that.

If you prefer, you can start the body scan at the top of your head and work your way down. Some people like to imagine that the wave of awareness is like the water in a shower flowing down along their body. You can do this version of the body scan quite quickly if you want to. And don't worry about remembering all the stages above. All you need to do is move your awareness through your body.

If you have areas of discomfort, stress or pain, imagine that you are breathing into the center of these areas and then move on. (If you encounter a pain or a discomfort that you have not come across before, consider seeking medical advice about it.) Even if you do encounter pain, the body scan helps you to understand that only part of your body is in pain. This is important because pain can hijack your attention and this hijacking can make the experience of pain worse than it needs to be.

Indeed, this principle can be applied beyond your body. It is probably safe to say you have difficulties in some areas of your life (we all do), while others are working well. If you focus only on the problems, your emotional state will be negative, perhaps even depressed; but give attention also to what's working well (as you do with physical sensations in the body scan) and your emotional state will lighten. You don't have to deny the difficulties, but by acknowledging what's positive as well as what's negative, you will create a more balanced feeling in which the negative may not loom so large anymore.

☼ IN A NUTSHELL: Scan your body with awareness from your feet up or your head down as a physical mindfulness practice that can help identify and lower tension.

A POINT OF PEACE

Calm your emotions and your thoughts by finding a point of peace in your body. How? By tuning in to where you feel most at peace physically and by bringing your attention to that place when you are seeking peacefulness.

If you wish, you can try right now to find that quiet place. Perhaps you might like to close your eyes if you're in a situation in which you can do so. Scan your body with your awareness. Look for a place that feels more peaceful and more calm than any other—a pool of quiet, so to speak. Imagine yourself breathing gently into that place. Imagine yourself spending a little time there. That's how you connect with that calm place inside your body. It is there for you whenever you need it.

○ IN A NUTSHELL: **Find that place in your body where you feel most at peace and take your attention to it whenever you need a sense of calm.**

In summary: The body is central to the practice of mindfulness. The practitioner of mindfulness makes a friend of his or her body and that, in turn, is reflected in a greater sense of peace in their life.

QUICK BODY SCAN

Practice: Become aware of your body, moving your awareness from the top of your head to your toes.

Commentary: In this practice you use your body to help you to be mindful. The body scan is a valuable practice, both in helping you to notice where you are tense and in helping you to relax that tension. Imagine the flow of awareness moving from your head to your toes, almost as though you're under a shower of awareness.

If you want to go deeper: If you notice any tension, imagine that you're breathing into it and then move on. After you have completed the quick body scan, remain at rest for a few moments before you go on with whatever you're doing.

NOTICE YOUR SHOULDERS

Practice: Bring your attention to your shoulders every now and then. Relax them. Then allow them to relax a little more than they are relaxed already.

Commentary: When we lose awareness of what is going on, we tend to lose awareness of our bodies as well. This is especially so when we are tense. That's when we raise our shoulders, scrunching them up as though we are getting ready to launch ourselves into battle. As soon as we become aware of our shoulders we realize what we are doing to them and we relax them. Do yourself a favor and bring your attention to your shoulders more often. You will be more mindful and you will waste less energy tensing them up unnecessarily.

If you want to go deeper: When you allow your shoulders to relax, also allow your spine to straighten a little. Experience this posture for a while and bring your breathing into your awareness as well.

MINDFUL FEET

Practice: Pay attention for a few moments to the sensation of your feet against the floor or the ground.

Commentary: To do this you have to come out of your mental chatter and into reality. If you're sitting, how lightly are your feet resting on the floor? If you're standing, are you relaxed or tensed? Do you notice a tingling sensation in the soles of your feet? Do your feet feel light against the floor or do they feel as though they are rooted? Either is good—this is just an awareness exercise. If you find it hard to focus on your breathing, bringing your attention to your feet is a good technique.

If you want to go deeper: Bring your attention to that tingling sensation in your feet for a while. Notice if the sensations are becoming stronger or fainter, if your feet are getting warmer or cooler.

MINDFULNESS OF POSTURE

Practice: Now and then become aware of your posture for a few moments.

Commentary: Becoming aware of your posture provides a very quick way to become mindful. It's especially helpful if you work in front of a computer, huddling into a screen with your muscles tensed up. It's also good for drivers who can so easily tense up their neck and shoulder muscles without noticing. But mindfulness of posture was practiced long before the invention of computers or the internal combustion engine. That's because the body isn't in the past or the future—it's here, in this present moment. And mindfulness of posture can bring an immediate sense of presence and calm.

If you want to go deeper: When checking your posture, do a quick scan of your body, noting areas of tension and of calm. Allow your body to settle into a sense of balance.

WASH YOUR HANDS

Practice: Wash your hands mindfully, feeling the sensation of the water and soap.

Commentary: This is a good example of an everyday activity that you can use to bring you into mindfulness. Most of us wash our hands many times a day and we often do it in a distracted sort of way. Try bringing awareness to the task, guiding your attention back if it wanders. Feel water, soap, the temperature of the water, the sensation of one hand washing the other. It is precisely because this is such a simple, practical, frequent, everyday act that washing your hands in awareness is such a useful mindfulness practice.

If you want to go deeper: As well as washing your hands mindfully, dry them mindfully. When you have finished, try to bring some of that sense of awareness to whatever you do next.

5

ON THE MOVE—MINDFUL COMMUTING AND BUSINESS TRAVEL

For many of us, to be a citizen of the world is to commute. Commerce is powered by, among other things, the legions of people who spend their time in cars, trains and planes on their way to meeting after meeting. The downside? Commuting can be stressful, tiring, boring and leave you feeling frazzled. But the good news is that by building mindfulness into your commute, you'll get there and back in better shape. You've still got to do it, sure, but with mindfulness packed in your bag, you'll make the whole experience a lot better than it would otherwise be. Here are some tips to help you become a mindful commuter and traveler.

IN THE CAR

Remember learning to drive? Remember how incredibly aware you were, hunched over the wheel, as the car reeled and lurched along the road? And how, over time, you became so competent and confident that you sometimes drove from A to B without having a clue as to how you got there? You vanished into your mind for the whole journey—or perhaps the car drove itself? Whatever the answer, it's quite scary to think how many people are driving along the roads right now with their attention anywhere but on their driving.

So mindful driving is a good thing. Not only does it provide an opportunity for awareness practice, it could also keep you alive. But if only driving were just about driving; all too often it's about inching forward in traffic jams, while frustration builds up in your mind and body. And while some of the exasperation of sitting in a traffic jam is inevitable, much of it is generated by the stories you tell yourself about how unfair it is that you are caught in this situation, how the world has conspired against you and how you might be late for that meeting. By practicing mindfulness of your breathing, however, bringing your attention back again and again to your posture or noticing what's going on in the world outside your car (and your head), you can help to break that spiral of negative and pointless thoughts.

Mindfulness can also help to prevent road rage, and does so in two different ways. First, people who get involved in road rage are often angry before the incident that triggers their outburst—but because mindfulness involves returning the attention again and again from a wandering mind and putting it instead on to actual reality, it is far less likely that they will stay caught up in angry thoughts in this way. Second, when, for example, the driver in front sits daydreaming as the light turns green and back to red again, you are likely, if you practice mindfulness, to realize that this is annoying, but it isn't the end of the world. You notice your frustration and your thoughts, but you don't give the incident more importance than it deserves.

Here are a few mindfulness tips for drivers:

Notice what's happening with your body. Quickly scan your body and especially your shoulders and neck for tension. Have you noticed that as you drive, tension seems to build up until it becomes so painful that you finally have to pay it attention? Give a little of your awareness to what's going on in your shoulders or the back of your neck. This can help you to avoid tensing up and can conserve your energy for whatever you need to do at the end of the journey.

What's going on in the mirrors? A lot goes on back there, you know, and by law you are supposed to continuously check it out. But when you go into a sort of trance behind the wheel, whatever is happening in the side or rearview mirrors may as well be happening on Mars—except that it's not, and you could end up getting a rude awakening. Using your mirrors as a mindfulness reminder makes a lot of sense.

What's happening on the road ahead? Way back in the days when cars were new, the roads were almost empty and speeds were relatively low, there were nevertheless a surprising number of fatalities. And this was because drivers had not yet realized the importance of anticipating what might be coming around a bend or from over that rise. Being alert to what is happening on the road ahead is a basic driving survival skill, but how alert are most of us, really? How aware are we of what's happening up ahead? Staying mindful of what's in front of you may keep you alive. On a less important but related note, have you ever noticed how easy it is to miss the fact, until you're almost upon them, that there's a policeman or policewoman standing on the side of the road in full view with a speed camera? That's a tribute to our habit of driving with only a dim awareness of what's in front of our eyes.

Can you feel the steering wheel? Noticing the movement of the steering wheel is a good way to be mindful in the car. So is noticing the feeling of the floor against your feet or the movement of windshield wipers in the rain.

○ IN A NUTSHELL: Stay mindful in the car by tuning in to how your body feels and by intentionally noticing what's happening on the road, both in front of and behind you.

ON THE PLANE

With the constant "ding-dongs," beeping noises, announcements, rattling carts and safety routines you might wonder how you can possibly be mindful on a plane—an environment that seems to be built to distract, bore and cramp. It can be done, though; just try these few tips:

Connect with your posture. Notice your feet against the floor, your back against the back of the seat. Notice what your hands are doing. Just noticing will help you to relax. What if you're cramped? If you encounter an area of tension, rest your attention on it and watch it soften.

Practice a little mindfulness of breathing. Follow your out-breath all the way out and allow the in-breath to occur absolutely without effort. This is especially useful if you are trying to catch a snooze.

Listen to a mindfulness meditation. Listening to a ten-minute mindfulness practice on the phone could help you get to your destination in good shape and in a mellow mood. You'll find some good mindfulness apps for smartphones listed at the end of this book and you can also download free audios from my website (www.padraigomorain.com).

Practice returning from the announcements to your breathing. If the announcements are distracting you from reading or working, practice returning awareness to your breathing after each one. And, yes, given the number of announcements on any flight, this means you'll get in a lot of mindfulness-of-breathing practice.

✿ IN A NUTSHELL: Connecting with your posture and breathing, as well as using mindfulness exercises stored on your phone or tablet, can reduce the effects of the hassle of air travel.

ON THE TRAIN

Taking a long journey by train still has quite a romantic image, but the reality of making regular train trips—whether short or long—can be very different. Trains are often crowded and noisy, making for a sometimes unpleasant experience. In these circumstances, a little mindfulness can get you to the end of your journey in a calmer mood than might otherwise have been the case. By all means read or listen to music if you prefer, but a mindful pause now and then to connect with your breath between chapters and tracks can be restful and refreshing. Here are some mindfulness practices that you can use at intervals during your journey.

Listen to the sound of the train. Modern trains don't chug along like the old, romantic steam engines, but they still run to a rhythm. So tune out of all that is going on inside the railway carriage or on your laptop or phone and rest your attention for a little while on the rhythm of the train.

Look at the passing scene as if for the first time. Have you noticed that on your first couple of journeys you may appreciate the passing scenery, but pretty soon you take it for granted? In fact, for most of us, if the railway company papered over the windows so that we could not see out, it would make no difference at all. So why not try, now and then, connecting mindfully with the passing scene instead of just recycling boring thoughts in your mind? Notice that in this case you are coming back to awareness of the scene as a mindfulness practice—it's just another way of being mindful.

Connect with your anchor point. Earlier I recommended that you notice where in your body you are most aware of your breathing. This could be at the tip of your nose, inside your nostrils, in your chest, tummy or elsewhere, and you can use this point to connect you with the experience of mindfulness at any time. So from time to time on your train journey, connect with your anchor point and notice your breathing there for a while. You'll find that on a crowded train this can actually give you a very welcome sense of space.

◯ IN A NUTSHELL: Listening to the rhythm, observing the passing scenery and connecting with your breathing can bring you to the end of your train journey feeling fresher than if you'd gone into a commuter trance.

IN THE HOTEL

Business travel means hotels. And very quickly, these can all blend into one forgettable blur, so try the following mindfulness practices as part of your hotel experience.

At reception. Can you remember the name of the receptionist? Sales people probably pick up on this sort of thing right away, but for most of us it requires an effort to be that mindful. So noticing a receptionist's name can be a mindfulness practice in itself.

One minute of mindfulness of breathing. Clear your head by taking a minute to be mindful of your breathing. But where? Sit on the side of the bed and focus your attention on the breath for about a minute. (Don't worry about getting the time right, you can just guess.) Return your awareness to the breath whenever your mind wanders.

Have a morning ritual. Whether or not you welcome the arrival of morning, a little mindfulness ritual will help get your day off to a good start. This can be as simple as forming the intention to be mindful as you're getting out of bed. Then follow up by opening the curtains, noticing what the sky is like and paying attention to your breathing as you brush your teeth or wait for the kettle to boil. This mindfulness ritual makes for a better way of starting your day than by cursing the fact that you have to get up!

Notice breakfast. I don't know about you, but something about the hotel breakfast experience turns me off. Sitting in a room full of strangers eating politely usually sets my teeth on edge in the mornings. But a little attention to the taste and aroma of your food can be helpful in this situation, as can awareness of your posture and your breathing.

Take a walk. If you stay in the same hotel regularly, seek out a pleasant place to take a walk. A familiar, mindful, enjoyable walk can give you a sense of belonging and can also provide a good interval for awareness and presence before you go on to meetings and other business.

◌ IN A NUTSHELL: Think of ways to make routine hotel stays mindful: a morning ritual, a walk (if you regularly stay in the same hotel), paying attention to your food and doing a little mindfulness of breathing in your room, for instance.

In summary: Commuting shouldn't be dead time, since we do so much of it in our lives. Whatever you do to make the journey less of a drag, including mindfulness as a strategy will keep your energy up and your levels of stress down. Try it next time you are on a busy train or in the car.

MINDFUL WAITING

Practice: When waiting in line, pay attention to this experience without passing judgment on what's happening. Instead, put your awareness lightly on your breath, on the soles of your feet or on any tightness in your stomach.

Commentary: Notice how difficult it is not to pass judgment on the person who's holding up the line or on the institution in question for having the audacity to force you to wait. See how quickly the judging part of the mind goes to work. If you put your attention on your tummy, you will probably notice your muscles tensing up. This is an excellent opportunity to train yourself to take control of your attention and to be less reactive to minor events. We get to stand in line a lot in this world, so instead of seeing queuing as dead time, use the experience to practice mindfulness.

If you want to go deeper: You're probably going to feel impatient in the line, even though you're practicing mindfulness. Try to observe your thoughts without getting caught up in their grumblings. Apply this to call-center waits, as well as physical ones.

JUST A MINUTE

Practice: Try to connect, for a minute, with whatever is going on around you.

Commentary: A minute is made up of many experiences: sounds, sights, light, shadow, temperature and sensation, to name but a few. It's good to come out of your mind sometimes and allow yourself to notice these experiences. What do you hear? See? What's the lighting like? What is your body connecting with—a seat, a wall, a bus stop? That's your life going on around you. Give your life the honor of paying a little attention to it now. In other words, be mindful of your life.

If you want to go deeper: Allow yourself to have a sense of settling into that minute, of allowing your body to settle into it, and become still as you do so.

EVERYDAY OBJECTS

Practice: In your home or your office, deliberately pause and look at everyday objects to which you have paid no attention for years.

Commentary: Sometimes, when you're filling in a form online, certain buttons are "grayed-out," meaning you can't do anything with them. It is likely that innumerable objects in your home or workspace are also grayed-out—you haven't really paid any attention to them for years. For instance, the plate you use every day may have a beautiful design that you haven't seen since shortly after you bought it. Isn't it scary to think how much of your one and only life is grayed-out? Use mindfulness of everyday objects to freshen your experience of your world.

If you want to go deeper: Wander around your home for a while and appreciate the designs on cups, plates, cutlery, wallpaper, carpets, curtains, vases and other objects.

YOUR MINDFUL PLACE

Practice: Choose a space in your environment in which you will be mindful whenever you are there.

Commentary: What's a space you are in every day? Kitchen? Bathroom? Bedroom? A mindful space doesn't have to be secluded and it doesn't matter if you can't light candles or burn incense in there. For most of us, for instance, the kitchen makes a really good mindful place. How does it work? You decide that whenever you're in the kitchen you'll be mindful. The kitchen, in this case, will become the room in which you get relief from the endless spinning of your mind.

If you want to go deeper: Choose a space at home, at work and outside and decide that whenever you are in one of those spaces you will cultivate awareness of what you are physically doing. Then, when appropriate (which may mean when you are alone), slow down your actions while you are in that space.

THE ART OF WAITING

Practice: When you're waiting for something to happen today—a kettle to boil, a bus to arrive, say—see if you can pass a minute or two without distracting yourself.

Commentary: We seem to be losing the capacity to wait calmly. Instead we turn immediately to our phones, as if the world's governments had passed a law against doing nothing. As time goes on, the rush to fill all possible spaces of time with activity seems to become more frantic. Some people have even been found to send texts in their sleep! Waiting could give us little pools of quiet in the long series of demands on our time. Waiting, in other words, could provide periods of renewal that we badly need.

If you want to go deeper: Clear your mind, notice what's going on in your body and allow yourself to sink into those moments of waiting. Instead of trying to figure out the shortest line in the supermarket or the bank, look for the longest and relax.

CHOOSE
A MINDFULNESS CUE

Practice: Pick a routine daily activity that you normally do without much awareness. Decide that in future you will pay attention to this activity as a means of bringing yourself into mindfulness.

Commentary: Because our minds continually drift away, mindfulness cues are immensely helpful in returning us to awareness of our flow of experience. To use mindfulness cues, pick one or two things you do habitually and decide that in future you will do them mindfully—this could be using an elevator or stairs, brushing your teeth, taking a shower, drinking that coffee you bought on the way in to work, lacing/unlacing your shoes, walking to your front gate or leaving the building in which you live. Then let this activity bring you back to mindfulness every time you do it.

If you want to go deeper: As you carry out this activity, slow down. Notice your posture, your reactions and what you see and hear.

6

MINDFUL EATING

E at mindfully and the experience of eating will be more enjoyable and healthy.

HOW CAN MINDFULNESS IMPACT MEALTIMES?

As you will see further on in this chapter, mindful eating will help you get more pleasure out of your food, will make it much easier to eat enough, but not too much, and will help you to avoid wolfing down lots of food to control negative emotions. Moreover, it will help you to spot any unhelpful attitudes you may have around food. That awareness, in itself, is a very big step toward addressing any food- or diet-related issues.

Let's start with a very simple practice to bring mindfulness to your eating.

The mindful minute at the table. This is a powerful tactic I always recommend to people and is the key to all the benefits I just outlined. It involves simply deciding that for at least the first minute of each meal, you will notice that you're actually eating and what you're eating; in other words, that you will pay attention to the taste, texture and aroma of your food. And when you're drinking tea or coffee or a glass of wine, notice each sip that you take. You'll enjoy it far more than if you were just pouring it down your throat.

This straightforward exercise will increase your appreciation of your food and you may even find that you can become attentive to food for longer than a minute. I'm not asking you to perform the Japanese tea ceremony, but to learn to build moments of awareness and mindfulness into your relationship with food and drink.

◯ IN A NUTSHELL: **Bring taste back into your life by eating mindfully for at least the first minute of each meal.**

The one-minute chocolate/raisin experiment. Take a raisin or a small square of chocolate. I want you to spend at least *one minute* eating this tiny morsel. During this time, notice what the texture is like in your mouth, notice the aroma, notice what it feels like to bite into it. If it is melting, notice what it's like to allow it to melt. Get a sense of the sensations in your tongue and your mouth. Notice the temptation to wolf it all down in the first ten seconds. Strong, isn't it? An exercise like this can be a very pleasant and revealing mindfulness practice. Also, that one minute alone can tell you so much about your approach to eating. It can help you to pay a great deal more attention to your food in the future.

◯ IN A NUTSHELL: Sharpen your experience of eating with games such as the one-minute experiment.

Are you full? Had enough? Then it's time to tell your brain you are full. For most of us, at some stage, our stomachs tell our brains that we are full and that it's OK to stop eating. But when you eat in a distracted or frantic way, you may already have eaten much more than you needed by the time that signal gets to your brain. This is especially likely to happen if you eat too quickly.

The signal is normally sent about twenty minutes after you start eating, so slow down and be mindful of your eating, you've got lots of time. You'll not only get to enjoy your food more, you'll also get to "full" with enough, rather than too much, food. In this way, mindfulness can contribute toward having a healthy diet without your actually having to go on a diet.

◯ IN A NUTSHELL: Eating mindfully slows you down, which gives your stomach time to tell your brain you've had enough.

Eating your emotions. Eating is an emotional act. Technically, we might see it simply as a way of removing our hunger, but I think we all know the story is more complex than that. Why else do we eat as a substitute for doing a task that makes us nervous or when we're bored, anxious, angry or sad? And it's not all negative: having a pleasant meal with good friends is a warming and cheering act. Even when we are alone, making an enjoyable meal for ourselves is an affirmation that we actually like ourselves and that we think we matter enough not to have to eat our dinner out of a tin. Of course, the flip side is that people sometimes eat too little or too much because they dislike themselves so much. We all know that anorexia, bulimia and other such conditions are intensely psychological.

So what does all this have to do with mindfulness? If you're mindful about your eating, you begin to notice patterns such as eating when you're not hungry or not bothering to prepare a pleasant meal when you're alone. Sometimes these can be bad habits left over from the past and you can drop them easily enough. At other times the patterns may reflect issues you need to address in your life. For instance, if you are lonely, maybe you need to contact somebody instead of "eating your loneliness."

○ IN A NUTSHELL: Look out for emotional eating. Find a better way to deal with anxiety, loneliness and other triggers.

Less mouth, more stomach. Usually, your stomach is your best guide as to whether you're hungry. Obvious, isn't it? Yet how often do we make the mistake of consulting our minds and not our stomachs?

And because so much eating is emotional, our minds can claim to be hungry even when our stomachs are not. For example, it's 11 a.m.: that means it's time for coffee and a chocolate bar. But maybe your stomach doesn't want any of that right now? Maybe you could wait until your stomach is actually hungry? Similarly, you can look at a mouthwatering display of food and notice that—well, your mouth is watering. Yet you may find your stomach is entirely content with what it has already had. And it can work the other way around too: your stomach may be hungry when you *think* it should be full because you ate something out of a cardboard box before you left for work this morning . . .

See how using your mind or your salivating mouth as the yardstick can take you straight out of touch with reality? A way to avoid this is to practice awareness of what your stomach is telling you. Notice how your stomach feels when you are eating or thinking about food. If you're already following other mindfulness practices in this book you will be quite used to the idea of attending to how your stomach is breathing, for instance, so this should be easy to do.

◌ IN A NUTSHELL: If you want to know whether you're hungry, tune in to your stomach, not your mind or your mouth.

Divorcing enjoyment from eating. Have you ever spent money on an expensive dish and allowed your mind to wander so much while you were eating it that you wondered if it had been worth the cost? That's the trouble with being inattentive to what we are putting on our plates and into our mouths. Why spend money, time and effort on food, only to ignore it when it comes to eating it? (This is also true of other aspects of our lives: we frequently allow distractions and inattentiveness to prevent us from appreciating what is in front of us.)

You can bring enjoyment back into your relationship with food by paying attention. This does not mean you have to sit in grim silence—it's simply a question of knowing you're eating when you're eating and appreciating what your food really tastes like. So getting more pleasure out of eating needn't be a matter of spending more money; by simply giving attention to what you already have, mindfulness can be more enriching than an expensive dish.

◌ IN A NUTSHELL: Increase your enjoyment of food by knowing you're eating when you're eating.

SHOPPING FOR FOOD

If you see yourself as having a problem with eating too much, you might do well to remember that mindful eating starts in the shopping aisle. Food shops and supermarkets are carefully designed and laid out with the aim of making you buy as much food as you can be persuaded to buy. Hardly surprising: that's how they make money. So when you spot that display of chocolate bars beside the cash register, it's not you versus the chocolate bars, it's you versus the wiles of the marketing industry.

Mindful shopping. Staying mindful in the grocery store can make a difference to both your bottom line and your waistline. Remain aware of what you went in there to buy—of what you need and don't need. Will the food in that tempting display just get thrown out of your fridge in three days' time? Does it serve you best to buy the large size or the medium size or the small size? Do you want the processed version or the one that involves you doing some cooking in the kitchen? A little mindfulness of your breathing as you're walking through the store will help keep your feet on the ground and your mind on track. That way, you will buy what you really want—not what you have been fooled into thinking you want.

◯ IN A NUTSHELL: Mindful shopping for food (knowing why you're buying what you're buying) is a great step toward better eating. It will also save you money.

In summary: If we ate only to remove our hunger we wouldn't have a problem with eating. But the simple act of eating can have so many associations for people, and very often we eat too much or without attention and fail to enjoy our food. Mindfulness of eating, on the other hand, can change our relationship with food and enhance the experience of eating and of living.

TASTE YOUR FOOD

Practice: Next time you are eating, notice what your food tastes like against your tongue.

Commentary: Food eaten without awareness is still nourishing (assuming it was nourishing to begin with), but we miss out so much on the enjoyment of food when we eat as though we're in a trance or when we wolf it down. We can be so out of touch with taste that we need to eat quite strong or sharp foods to get a kick out of eating. Noticing the taste and the aroma (which contributes to the taste) opens up a whole new world of sensation to us. It is also likely to slow down our eating, so that we do not consume more than we want.

If you want to go deeper: Take a small square of chocolate or a raisin and see if you can spend two minutes eating it, with awareness of taste, texture and any aroma. Notice how strong the temptation is to wolf it down. Notice how much more you experience when you slow down the process and eat mindfully.

URGE SURFING

Practice: Next time you feel hungry, notice what that's like for a little while before you eat. Connect with the physical sensation. Where is it in your body? Does it rise and fall in intensity? Does it cover a large or a small area?

Commentary: We are, in many ways, creatures of habits and urges. Those who are most at the mercy of their urges have the least control over their lives. But urges rise and fall, and becoming aware of an urge as it does so opens a space in which to make a choice to satisfy it or not. Eating healthily is essential, but we all have urges to do things that are not helpful to us. Seeing the urge rise and fall without having to satisfy it—urge surfing—is a useful skill. Practice on the urge to eat—but then eat what you need.

If you want to go deeper: Sit still for a time and notice the nature of the urge, as above. Notice how it changes. Rather than seeing yourself as resisting the urge, see yourself as observing it while creating space for choices.

DRINK YOUR TEA

Practice: Next time you're drinking a cup of tea (or coffee) be aware of at least the first minute of the experience.

Commentary: Of the billions of cups of tea and coffee drunk in the world every day, many are drunk with little or no awareness. That's a pity—a missed opportunity to enjoy one of the day's small pleasures. Bringing even a minute of awareness to the experience helps build a mindfulness practice into your day while doing something you were going to do anyway. And it means you get more value out of those increasingly expensive teas and coffees.

If you want to go deeper: Pay attention to taste and aroma. Think of the millions of other people who are having a tea or coffee right now and decide that you will be among those who do so in awareness.

SLOW FOOD

Practice: When preparing food for yourself, do it slowly.

Commentary: Lots of people put more care into preparing food for others than for themselves. That's a pity. Preparing your food mindfully is a statement in itself—namely, that you deserve to have your food prepared with care. Even if what you're preparing is convenience food, you can still choose mindfully in the shop and prepare mindfully in the kitchen. We work, partly, to eat, so it's a real contradiction if we then thoughtlessly throw our food into a microwave and slap it onto a plate. In mindfulness, you get to treat yourself as well as you would a guest.

If you want to go deeper: Deliberately slow down your food preparation. Consider the earth and the ocean from which your food originally came. After you have prepared it, eat your food with attention.

7

MINDFULNESS AT HOME

Mindfulness is all very well—but how are you supposed to do it in a busy home? Actually, you will find innumerable opportunities to build mindfulness into your home life. We will look here at ways in which any of us can use home routines to help us practice mindfulness. Later in this chapter I also include tips for mindful parenting.

MINDFULNESS IN THE MORNING

Let's begin at the beginning, with your early-morning routine.

Mindfulness morning rituals. If you want to be mindful during the day, form the intention to be so from the get-go in the morning. Intention, it is said, is the point of the needle: where the point goes, everything else follows. So before your feet hit the floor, tell yourself, "I will be mindful today." And whether you leap around the bedroom full of energy or shuffle around rubbing the sleep out of your eyes, it doesn't matter—just practice being aware of your leaping or shuffling, noticing your feet against the floor, maybe even your breathing, and that's mindfulness.

It's very easy to build other little mindfulness rituals into the start of your day:

- Do you pick up your smartphone as your very first act of the morning? If so, give a little of your awareness to your breathing or to your posture as you check messages, texts and emails. That simple act of self-awareness will help you to avoid being sucked into a storm of negative thoughts, especially if you are faced with an annoying communication from an annoying person. Do you put on the kettle and make a cup of tea or coffee? Make a point of noticing that the kettle starts to warm up when you press the switch (you'd notice if it didn't). I like to sit and observe my thoughts without comment while the coffee machine gurgles away. It doesn't gurgle for long but somehow, even that pause seems to give me a better handle on the day.

- Make a point of noticing water splashing on your hands while checking, with awareness, what's happening outside the door or the window—see how the trees or plants are doing—or listen to morning sounds from the street or the road. Pause for a moment.

- Even something as simple as putting your shoes on can be a mindful practice if you slow down and put your attention on what you're doing.

Mindfulness gets even a tough day off to a better start. If you think it is too hard to do when you have a difficult day ahead, I can assure you that paying attention to what's going on in the moment is a great alternative to grumbling to yourself about what the day has in store.

○ IN A NUTSHELL: Start your day mindfully by doing at least one of your early-morning activities in awareness. It will stand you in good stead for the rest of the day.

DURING THE DAY

Can you think of daytime activities you normally carry out with your mind a million miles away? Pick out one or two of these and choose to do them in awareness in future. In this way, they will give you little mindfulness opportunities throughout your day.

Everyday mindfulness opportunities. Pay attention while you are doing the washing-up, as you lift each glass out of the soapy water or as your hands touch the hot water. Bring your mind back to the present whenever it wanders from the task. You can also do this when you are:

- brushing your teeth
- looking out the window first thing in the morning
- drinking tea
- starting the car
- using the elevator at work
- starting up your computer
- entering passwords
- taking a shower
- emptying or filling the dishwasher
- gardening
- hanging clothes on the line

- answering the doorbell

- entering or leaving your workplace

- walking up or down stairs

- brushing your hair

IN A NUTSHELL: Any of the above, and more, can be done mindfully. Choose one or two activities as part of your daily mindfulness practice.

Mindful cooking and washing-up. Isn't cooking always mindful? No, it isn't. How often have you rushed preparing a meal, just to get it done, and ended up with something that really wasn't worth the effort? And how often does "cooking" mean no more than just stabbing the cling wrap on the plastic box, then jabbing the buttons on the microwave to get that over with too? How relaxed can your meal be in these conditions? And it's very likely that the TV will get more attention than the food and you might be as stressed at the end of the meal as you were at the start.

Would mindful food preparation improve your cooking? Probably (although I can't guarantee it)—but at the very least it will improve your mood. Pay attention as you chop the vegetables or stir-fry your ingredients. Observe the colors of the vegetables and the smells wafting from the pan. Bring your mind back to the present if it starts to wander. You'll see that food preparation can become a means of de-stressing in itself—and you'll certainly get more enjoyment out of the meal.

Would mindful cooking slow you down? Again, probably, although not necessarily and not to any significant degree. It's about clarity of mind, knowing what you're doing while you're doing it.

◯ IN A NUTSHELL: Preparing your meals in awareness of what you're doing will make for better food and will contribute to your mindfulness practice.

Mindful tidying. My dream is that a tech genius will invent an affordable robot that I can observe mindfully as it whirs around, restoring my space to a state of tidy spaciousness.

Meanwhile, however, I make the best of having to do it myself, and you can too. Have you noticed that items move (possibly while you are sleeping!) from where they belong to other places? Try moving these items back to their homes without grumbling about it in your mind. That's being mindful. Watch your reactions as you tidy. When you're about to get lost in memories about that souvenir on your shelf, see what it would be like to let the memories be and move on. Alternatively, see what it would be like to pick up the item and observe the emotions it calls up without getting lost in them. Then put it back and continue tidying. Tidying, as a mindfulness exercise, will also leave you with a neat, clean space—not a bad deal.

○ IN A NUTSHELL: Choose at least one aspect of tidying and decide to do that mindfully.

MINDFULNESS TO HELP YOU SLEEP

In our sleep-deprived era, one of the greatest benefits of mindfulness practice is that it can significantly improve your chances of a good sleep. Here are some mindfulness strategies for getting to sleep.

Start during the day. Some psychologists believe the brain uses sleep and dreaming to process the day's events. If they are right, then preoccupying ourselves with anxieties and resentments leaves a lot of work for the brain to do during sleep. This may explain why you can sometimes wake up tired after a night's sleep—your energy has been used by your brain as it works at filing away your worries and irritations. What this all comes down to is that a clear head during the day is conducive to a clear head, and better-quality sleep, at night. Practicing mindfulness will help you to achieve this.

Follow your out-breath. Withdraw attention from your worries by putting it on your out-breath. As I mention in Chapter 3 (where you can find much more on mindful breathing), the out-breath is especially relaxing and when you are in bed at night it can feel deep and pleasant. But what if your head is full of thoughts? You don't have to suppress your thoughts—in fact, thought suppression doesn't really work very well. Instead, when a thought comes up, gently move your attention back to the out-breath and do the same with any subsequent thoughts.

Label your thoughts or your breathing. When worrisome thoughts come to you, label them silently with the word "thinking" and return to your breathing. Labeling negative thoughts helps to quiet down the emotions associated with them. If you feel you need more than this, then as you breathe out, say silently, "breathing out"; as you breathe in, say silently, "breathing in."

Don't force your breathing, allow it. See if you can observe your breath rising and falling, instead of directing it. Observing your breathing in this way also helps take attention away from your worries. If you don't like observing your breathing, put your attention on your body. For instance, observe the feeling of your body against the mattress or the bedclothes.

Do a body scan. For many people the body scan is their favorite way to get to sleep at night or to fall back to sleep when they wake up. Sometimes you'll fall asleep during the first body scan, but it doesn't really matter whether you do or not—in my experience, even if the body scan doesn't send me to sleep, I still feel very rested when I get up in the morning. So simply repeat it slowly, and as often as you need to. I include instructions for the body scan in the chapter on mindfulness and the body (page 47). Allow yourself to take your time. You're in bed: there's no need to hurry. And as with the out-breath, whenever you drift into thought, return your attention to whatever part of your body you're currently focusing on.

"I'm still awake." Remember that this is a negative thought too and can be counterproductive. Practice returning not only from thoughts about your worries or annoyances, but also from the thought that you are not sleeping, that the night is passing you by, etc. It helps if you don't know what the time is and if you don't check it.

◯ IN A NUTSHELL: Mindfulness practices—especially the body scan—can help you to sleep and rest at night.

MINDFULNESS AND PARENTING

First question: Will your kids allow you to sit and meditate? The answer to this is probably sometimes yes, sometimes no. And this applies to most activities in which parents wish to engage. Luckily, as this book continually points out, you don't have to sit down and meditate to practice mindfulness, and when it comes to parenting, mindfulness on the go is the gold standard. That said, you can play some simple mindfulness games with small children (see below).

Maintaining an attitude of mindfulness yourself will be immensely valuable in dealing with the demands of parenting. If your attention vanishes into the busyness of parenting, you stand a good chance of ending the day in a state of physical and mental exhaustion. If you remain mindful as much as you can, however, you could go through the same busyness and meet the same demands and end the day in much better shape.

Pause for sanity. Taking a mindful pause—by connecting with your breath or with the feeling of your feet on the floor, for instance—can restore presence of mind to the most harassed parent. You'll find the mindful pause especially helpful when your child is whining or throwing a tantrum. The pause, which is like stepping back from the storm, will help you to ride out both whines and tantrums without throwing a tantrum yourself.

◯ IN A NUTSHELL: Practice a mindful attitude to help keep yourself in a (relatively) calm state when parenting.

MINDFULNESS FOR SMALL CHILDREN

Here are some mindful games you can use with small children (for mindfulness for teenagers, see the next chapter).

Toy on tummy. Your child lies down and places a favorite toy on his or her tummy and then moves the toy up and down by breathing in and out. The toy is "asleep" and the child must breathe gently so as not to wake it up. You might want to do this together with your child, in which case they can choose a toy for you to raise up and down with your tummy. Through doing this exercise, your child experiences a relaxed attention which is very much a part of mindfulness practice.

Balloon breathing. Ask your child to imagine a colorful balloon in his or her tummy. When they breathe in, the balloon gets bigger; when they breathe out, it gets smaller. Do this with your child a few times, describing the color of your balloon and asking your child to describe his or hers. This exercise encourages belly breathing, which is very relaxing.

Happy place. Invite your child to look for a happy place in his or her body. Perhaps a smile lives in this place. When your child finds their happy place, he or she can spend some time in it now and then: whenever they are upset or if they wake up during the night, they can imagine snuggling into the happy place with the smile. Take your child through this exercise when he or she goes to bed. This gives them a way of "being with" their emotions.

○ IN A NUTSHELL: You'll find lots of ways to help small children to be mindful and to have fun or relax at the same time—raising a favorite toy on their tummy by breathing in and out or finding a "happy place" in their body, for instance. It all helps kids to gain a little detachment from their thoughts and to cultivate positive feelings.

MINDFULNESS FOR OLDER CHILDREN

Older children (aged seven and upward) can learn almost all mindfulness techniques. These will stand them in good stead, not only during childhood, but for the rest of their lives. Try the exercises below with older children.

7/11 breathing. This exercise, which we looked at earlier (see p. 32), is popular with children and helps them to get used to turning to awareness of the breath, especially when emotions or anxieties are running high. It involves counting to seven on the in-breath and counting to eleven on the out-breath. Doing this two to three times immediately brings the child into the present moment and cultivates presence of mind. You, as a parent, could demonstrate this by counting as the child breathes and then getting the child to count as you breathe.

What animal? For this use a box of figures, such as animals or dolls or soldiers. Ask your child, "What are you thinking? If your thought was an animal (soldier, doll) which of these would it be?" The child chooses a figure and then asks you what you are thinking about and which figure your thought would be. The exchange goes on until you have used up all the figures in the box. Each of you then has to remember the thought represented by each figure, and whoever can remember the most wins. This game helps children to get a little distance from their thoughts and to see that thoughts don't always have to be acted upon or taken terribly seriously. As a bonus, you may learn a great deal about what is on your child's mind.

Body scan for children. Your child has an imaginary flashlight that shines a light down their body from head to toe. As the flashlight shines on each part of the body, your child imagines that part going to sleep. When the flashlight gets to the toes, your child must stay very quiet, so as not to wake up the body while it is having a snooze. This gives your child practice at moving from his or her thoughts to awareness of the body and this, in turn, can help with sleeping and relaxation.

◯ IN A NUTSHELL: Adapt adult mindfulness practices for children and do them along with your child. The body scan and 7/11 breathing are examples of this.

> **In summary:** The home provides many opportunities to practice mindfulness without having to shut the bedroom door to meditate. You can do that too if you want to, but if you don't, the mindful ideas in this chapter will be really useful. If you practice mindfulness, give your children a lifelong resource by teaching them to do so as well. Mindfulness practice helps immensely with the demands of parenting and you can find many ways, including adapting the ideas here, to pass on this practice to your children.

MORNING KITCHEN MINDFULNESS

Practice: When you walk into your kitchen in the morning, notice that lights come on and the kettle boils when you press the switches.

Commentary: All you are doing here is noticing actions that you actually carry out every day, but often with your mind on something else. The something else may be that meeting coming up at work or an email you need to send. By carrying out these habitual actions in mindfulness, you lift your head above that deluge of thoughts—perhaps worries—that can so easily flood in first thing in the day. This practice need take no more than a few moments.

If you want to go deeper: As you wait for the kettle to boil or for the coffee machine to do its magic, sit down and put your attention on your breathing. In this way, you will deepen your mindfulness practice and strengthen your "mindfulness muscle" while your first tea or coffee of the day is on its way.

ACKNOWLEDGE
COMPLETION

Practice: Step out of the endless cycle of activity to acknowledge the tasks you have completed today.

Commentary: Our relentless focus on what's next reduces our sense of satisfaction in things done, keeps our stress levels up and drags us out of the present and into an always-demanding future. Every now and then, climb out of the stream onto the bank for a while. Quietly acknowledge what you have done before you dive into the swim again. You are not just a future-machine. Take this moment to recall a few of the things you have completed today—even getting out of your warm bed counts!

If you want to go deeper: Before you go to sleep tonight, think of some tasks—big or small—that you have completed today. Take a moment to acknowledge your efforts. When your mind goes off into a series of "what ifs" and "if onlys," bring it back to that acknowledgment.

8

MINDFULNESS FOR TEENAGERS

Teenagers around the world are beginning to realize the benefits of mindfulness in their daily lives. Later, I outline some mindfulness practices that will show you, as a teenager, how to keep returning your attention to the present moment. You can do this through awareness of your breathing, of your walking or by other means that work for you. Coming back to the present moment whenever your attention drifts away, or whenever you get lost in emotions, is the essence of mindfulness.

Before we look at those practices, though, let's consider some of the benefits.

THE BENEFITS OF MINDFULNESS
FOR TEENAGERS

- **Worry less.** Teenagers can spend a lot of time worrying about the past and the future, and while we all have to make sense of the past and think about the future, the present is where we live and act. When you practice mindfulness, you spend more time in the present—made up of sights, sounds, physical sensations, smells and people. You can always get back to the present when you start to worry by bringing your attention back to your breathing.

- **Stress less.** When you're stressed out or feeling bad you can use mindfulness to help you to step back from that feeling and to see it without getting swept away by it. It's like being able to stand on a beach and watch the waves without letting them carry you off.

- **Become more attentive and improve concentration.** Do you find it difficult to keep your attention on what you're doing? Practicing mindfulness will improve your ability to focus. That's because it involves bringing your attention back again and again to whatever is going on for you right now. This is like training an attention muscle. Knowing how to focus your attention is a really valuable skill both now and in the future and mindfulness provides that focus.

- **Slow down.** We live in a busy world and sometimes it can feel as though everything is happening too fast. Not only that, but sometimes you can feel that you yourself are doing things too quickly. When you practice mindfulness by coming to the present more often, you can sometimes get a sense of time slowing down. It's not quite slow motion, but a little slowing that can help you to gather your wits about you. For this reason, mindfulness makes it much easier for you to do one thing at a time without always running ahead of yourself.

- **Reduce impatience.** When you feel impatient, you're really looking to get away from the present moment into the future—even if only a couple of minutes into the future. If you practice mindfulness, you'll feel far less need to escape from the present; it involves being willing to stay in the present (which will become the future anyway, if you wait!). Why does this matter? When people spend all their time thinking about the next thing they're going to do, it can be difficult to enjoy what's happening right now. And then, when they go on to the next thing, they'll be jumpy and restless because they're focused on the next thing after that. Mindfulness helps you get more out of your present experiences, while still being aware of the things that you are working toward.

- **Choose to feel better.** Choosing to be mindful is like choosing to feel better. That's because usually mindfulness will help you to feel calmer and more in control of yourself. Will it make you happy? Nothing can guarantee happiness at any given time—it is sometimes said that happiness is like a butterfly that lands on your hand unexpectedly and flutters away when you notice it. But while you cannot switch happiness on and off, mindfulness will help you to feel better more of the time.

- **Control anger.** When you are angry, you will often find that your anger gets worse the more you think about it. When you're mindful, you can feel what your anger is like physically—for example, some people (including myself) feel their bodies heating up. If you put your attention on that physical sensation, but stay out of your thoughts, the anger will die down. That's because physical sensations always die down if you give them a little time.

- **Keep a cool head for exams.** Exams are one unfortunate reality of teenage life. The mindfulness tips below can help you to stay calm and focused both when preparing for and during the exam. That's because mindfulness will encourage you to return your attention again and again to what you are doing right now; and this is so much more helpful than getting lost in scary stories in your imagination about what might happen. For instance, when you are making a study plan, mindfulness can help you to stick with the planning, rather than worrying about the future. Remember: The work you do right now at the desk you're sitting at right now is what matters.

- **Cultivate better friendships.** Teenagers who practice mindfulness also seem to get along better with their friends and with other people in general because it helps them to cultivate a greater fellow-feeling with others.

☁ IN A NUTSHELL: By returning your attention to the present moment again and again you will benefit from the calming and steadying effects of mindfulness.

Emotions in your teenage years. I don't suppose it is news to you that your teenage years can be very turbulent. Not only are you creating your identity, but emotions can be overwhelming. It's hardly surprising then that this period of adolescence is sometimes referred to as the "storm and stress" years. Our capacity to regulate our emotions doesn't develop fully until we reach our early twenties. However, because mindfulness helps to strengthen the links between the thinking brain and the emotional brain it is especially helpful for teenagers in helping to cool down emotions and in creating a space in which to consider your response before you react. It also gives you a completely new way to coexist with your emotions. When you find yourself flooded by emotions you can move to awareness of breathing or of walking, for instance, and this gives you that all-important space.

◌ IN A NUTSHELL: Practice mindfulness by returning your awareness to your breathing, say, to get a space in which to handle strong emotions.

7/11 breathing. Teenagers find 7/11 breathing (see p. 32) to be a very useful practice that they can bring anywhere: the classroom, sports field and interactions with the family. It can also help to deal with stress while studying. The longer out-breath is very calming, which is why it makes such a good mindfulness practice.

◌ IN A NUTSHELL: Pause and count to seven while you breathe in and to eleven while you breathe out.

Following the out-breath. Follow your breath all the way down to the floor (see p. 32). Even though the out-breath is really leaving through your nose or mouth, it can feel as though it's going down through your body, into the earth. Notice how that feels and then wait for your body to breathe in again by itself. Do this as often as you like.

◯ IN A NUTSHELL: Following your out-breath all the way out is a good way to calm yourself.

Labeling. Whenever you feel carried away by thinking or by emotions, label that with the word "thinking" and bring your attention back to your breathing or to your feet against the floor. Saying "thinking" and then bringing your attention back to your breathing cools emotions down. You'll find more on labeling on page 144.

◯ IN A NUTSHELL: To calm down emotions, label them with the word "thinking" and return to whatever else you're doing.

Mood surfing. Would you like to be able to control your moods? Well, the bad news is that moods are largely outside our control, but the good news is that they don't have to dictate our behavior. You can learn to stay with moods as they rise and fall away, without acting on them—to allow them to come and go, notice that feeling of anger, sadness, loneliness or whatever it might be, then switch your attention to your breathing or to an activity like walking while you wait for the mood to change. Sometimes, it also helps if you can picture what your mood is like because that gives you some distance from it. Here are some ways to do this: Notice where in your body you feel your mood. Does the mood get bigger or smaller? Is it dark or bright? If it were a color, what color would that be? Is it a very tightened-up mood or is it loose and relaxed? See your mood as an image. Could your mood be like a cloud? Is it a dark cloud or a bright one? Could it be a wave in the sea? What kind of wave? Gentle or very strong? Could your mood be a sound? What sort of sound? If it's music, what sort of music?

○ IN A NUTSHELL: You can "surf" your moods by watching them and waiting while they rise and fall.

Awareness of posture. Instead of awareness of breathing, some people prefer mindfulness of posture—in other words, an awareness of the fact that they are sitting, standing, walking, running or lying down. Try awareness of your posture, for instance, next time you're sitting in the classroom and you will find your concentration improves. Awareness of your posture can also give you a mental space when you're in an examination, and that space can be very useful in helping you to concentrate on reading questions and working out answers.

◌ IN A NUTSHELL: Bringing your awareness to your posture takes you out of your racing thoughts, especially in stressful situations.

Finding your anchor point. Can you pause for a moment and notice where in your body you are aware of your breathing? This might be at the end of your nose, in your chest or at the back of your throat. When you find that point, you can become mindful at any time by putting your attention on it. This is one of the quickest ways you will find to be mindful and it's useful in any situation in which you might feel pressured: at home, in school or with your peer group, for instance. For more, see page 30.

◌ IN A NUTSHELL: Identify where in your body you most feel your breath and bring your attention to that point when you want to be mindful. The more often you do this, the more effective it will be as a gateway into mindfulness.

Mindful walking. Walking is a really good way to be mindful, especially if you're feeling emotional or upset in any way—perhaps following a disagreement with friends. You'll find more on mindful walking on page 53 but essentially it means noticing your feet on the ground as you're walking along, or noticing your arms moving—in other words, bringing your attention back again and again to your walking.

◌ IN A NUTSHELL: Walking with awareness that you are walking is a great way to be mindful.

MINDFULNESS REMINDERS

It's really helpful to have ways of remembering to be mindful. So try listing some ordinary, routine activities that you do without even thinking, then decide that whenever you're doing them, you will remember to be mindful. Some examples might be brushing your teeth, going to your locker in school, brushing your hair, texting, entering passwords, walking through the front door of your home or any other everyday action you can think of.

The idea is to pick one or two of these (that should be plenty) that you will perform in awareness that you are doing them. This will remind you to come out of your thoughts and emotions for a moment.

◌ IN A NUTSHELL: **Pick a routine activity, like brushing your teeth, and decide to do it mindfully as a way to remember to practice mindfulness.**

In summary: I hope this chapter has given you a flavor of what mindfulness can bring to your life and how it can be of enormous help to you as you navigate your teenage years and beyond. If you want to pursue mindfulness further, you will find lots of ideas elsewhere in this book—the calendar on p. 175, for example, is a great reference point for a daily mindfulness thought or practice. You can also find lots of mindfulness practices on YouTube. The main thing to remember is that by using one or two favorite exercises from this chapter, you can experience the benefits of mindfulness every day.

JUST LOOK

Practice: Look at the space around you without judging or commenting. Now pick out an object within the space and look without judging or commenting.

Commentary: The mind works by association. When you look at a space, an object or a person the memories, fantasies, feelings and thoughts linked to whatever you're looking at become active and seek your attention. One of the effects of this is that you can easily reach a point where you see not the object, but its associations. So you may look at a person and see him or her through the lens of your past involvement with them. Meanwhile, you risk missing out on the actual, present-day human being. This exercise gives you a fresh look, and a more realistic view of your world.

If you want to go deeper: Consider something that has had a meaning for you for a long time—perhaps a photograph, a souvenir or even a room. Notice the various associations that come to mind as you look at it. Now return your attention to the thing itself.

THE SOUNDSCAPE

Practice: What can you hear right now in your vicinity? Can you listen without telling yourself a story about the sounds and without interpreting them? As you do this, if a story or interpretation comes into your mind, return your attention gently to the sounds.

Commentary: Our days are full of sounds we no longer hear—not, in the vast majority of cases, because we are deaf, but because we long ago stopped paying attention to them. Tuning in to everyday sounds now and then can be a good awareness exercise: combing or brushing your hair, putting a cup down on the table, turning the pages of a book or magazine, for instance. As always in mindfulness practice, return your attention to the sounds you are listening to whenever you notice it has drifted away.

If you want to go deeper: Practice spotting everyday sounds that have become so familiar you no longer hear them—the sound of your own breathing, of your friend's breathing, of doors opening or closing, of birds singing or water flowing. This exercise will bring you into a greater sense of awareness as you go through the day.

WHAT'S GOING ON?

Practice: Whether you are reading this at your desk, at a table or on a bus or train, pause for a few moments. Take in the sights and sounds around you, as if asking yourself "What's going on?"

Commentary: This mindful pause actually has a number of benefits. If you tense yourself up, perhaps around your shoulders and neck muscles, it will give you an opening to notice the tension and to relax it. If you are working on a problem for which you need to generate some creative ideas, the solution may now get a chance to come through from your subconscious and be heard. It also gives you an opportunity to step out of any racing of your thoughts.

If you want to go deeper: As you pause and look around, bring your awareness to your body, to your posture and to your breathing as well.

IMAGINARY DRAWING

Practice: Make an imaginary drawing of a familiar object. Look at the lines and shapes you would need to include in your drawing.

Commentary: To become mindful of the familiar, to see again, look at an object that has been part of your life for so long you barely notice it anymore. Allow your eyes to rest on the lines that would make up a drawing of the object. What spaces might you need to include? Does the object seem to have any sort of dynamic energy you might want to represent? The extent to which we become blind to objects and people in our environment is remarkable. This mindfulness exercise restores a sense of connection with your familiar world, the world where you spend your days.

If you want to go deeper: Draw the object or part of the object, remembering it's not about the quality of the finished product, but about the reawakening of your awareness. Or join the growing mindful photography trend and photograph the object, observing it first from a number of angles.

OTHERS' BREATHING

Practice: When you are speaking to another person for a while, pay attention to how that person is breathing.

Commentary: Observing another person's breathing keeps your attention on the conversation you are having with them. It provides an example of how listening is not just about hearing. The breath carries so much of our feeling and our history that to be aware of it is to communicate at a deep level beyond words. Some people are very obvious in how they breathe. Others are far more subtle. If you practice mindfulness, you already pay attention to your own breath. Extending that attention—without being obvious about it—to the breathing of another enhances the presence you bring to the encounter.

If you want to go deeper: In our time, we have many very rapid conversations. Try slowing down conversations a little to enable you to observe the breathing of the other person. This is a question of being present, instead of always operating out of How-soon-can-I-get-away? mode.

9

MINDFUL RELATIONSHIPS

Relationships are patterns. That's not all they are, but for our purposes it really helps to be aware that every relationship falls into a pattern. And the pattern translates into habits: habits of seeing, thinking about and talking to somebody in a particular way. Mindfulness, on the other hand, encourages us to step out of tired patterns and to see our relationships with new eyes, and this chapter will give you some ways to do just that.

THE MINDFUL PAUSE

There is great wisdom in the saying "Fools rush in where angels fear to tread." The angels, it seems, have learned the value of the mindful pause. A great deal of mindfulness practice involves pausing in the middle of the rush of life. But it might also involve pausing in the middle of your interaction with your partner. Here are a few examples:

- When you meet your partner at the end of the workday, pause to take in how they really are before you dish out a standard greeting.

- If you're about to criticize, pause to consider if, in the past, criticism has really achieved anything. Perhaps it often hasn't, in which case why make matters worse by criticizing now? Could you find a softer way to say what you want to say? Marriage researchers say that when we want to express a criticism of our partner we should start by expressing ourselves as softly and gently as we can, not harshly. It seems obvious, but it's ignored all too often. If you're being mindful in your interactions with your partner, however, you gain the space in which to choose to start off softly.

- According to marriage research, most of the long-term differences between partners are never resolved. So fighting over old, familiar issues is often a complete waste of time. Your partner may say something to you that is simply not worth the effort of arguing with, and you need to be able, now and then, to shrug off their negative opinion of you or of your behavior—like a dog shaking off water. This is different from stonewalling or becoming silently defensive, and mindfulness will help you to do it more easily.

- We have all, from time to time, had reason to wish that we had kept our mouth shut for a few seconds and not said something that made matters worse. Silence, we seem to have to keep reminding ourselves, is golden—even for the few seconds it takes to replace an unhelpful response with one that's more constructive. Practicing mindfulness cultivates the ability to spot the opportunity for that mindful pause before it's too late.

○ IN A NUTSHELL: A mindful pause before speaking or acting can change the entire tone of a relationship for the better.

LOOK AT YOUR PARTNER

Have you ever found that you can walk many times down a familiar street without noticing a particular feature until it is pointed out to you? That is the numbing effect of habit. And the same can happen with people. If you have been with your partner for a long time, consider whether you have actually looked at him or her lately. Have you really looked with full attention at this person who is accompanying you on your journey through your one and only life? Or are you looking at an old, faded picture of that person that's in your mind? Try looking at your partner with new eyes—in other words, with mindful eyes—and see what a difference it makes.

○ IN A NUTSHELL: Look at your partner, not through a filter (or blindfold) of previous experiences and patterns, but just look.

MINDFUL LISTENING

Do you remember a time when somebody really listened to you? It felt good at a very deep level, didn't it? And it isn't a question of what the other person can do for you, necessarily; the joy is simply in being heard and listened to with deep attention. That is exactly what mindful listening accomplishes. Here are some ways to listen mindfully to another person:

- Listen to what is being said, but without trying to figure out a reply in your own mind at the same time. Just listen.

- Think of yourself as listening with your attention and not with your ears.

- Speaking to somebody who doesn't even look at you is a horrible experience, but by listening mindfully, you can give someone the very reverse of that. Look at their face and eyes as they speak. I'm not talking, of course, about staring or glaring, but resting your attention on the other person's face and eyes as they speak. To keep your attention from wandering, if the other person has a lot to say, you could put, maybe, 10 percent of your attention on your breathing as you listen. It helps to anchor you and to maintain a friendly attention at the same time.

• Notice your own physical reactions as you listen to the person speaking. Sometimes, being aware of those reactions can make you far more aware of how you respond.

○ IN A NUTSHELL: Give other people the gift of mindful listening by paying attention to what they are saying and how they are saying it.

MINDFUL SPEECH

Have your words ever been misunderstood by your partner? Of course they have. Have your words ever hurt another person unintentionally? That too. Mindful speech is a matter of paying attention to what you're saying and how you're saying it. If you pay attention you'll notice that the words are helpful or unhelpful. You'll have a better chance of realizing you're about to say something that will make things worse, rather than better—or even that you have already said something that has made things worse, in which case that awareness alone gives you the opportunity to correct yourself.

◯ IN A NUTSHELL: Know what you are saying when you are saying it to make your speech helpful, rather than unhelpful.

RECYCLING RESENTMENTS AND HOW TO STOP IT

One of the behaviors that makes our life smaller and meaner is that of cultivating our resentments. Think of a sort of resentment triangle: one point is the memory of whatever it is that we resent; the second is the feeling of anger or even bitterness that it summons up; and the third is telling the story to ourselves again and again, reliving the scenes in our heads for the umpteenth time and telling ourselves what a rotten person the other individual is. That third point is the one that keeps the resentment going, and it can poison your life not only for days or weeks, but even for decades in some cases.

Can you stop resentments from arising? No. But a mindful approach is to accept that you can do little or nothing about the first two points of the triangle. Every so often, maybe even every day, you are going to be reminded of whatever it is that you resent. And that is going to summon up feelings that are unpleasant: feelings of anger, dismay or some other negative response. But when that happens, you can then quite deliberately decide that you will step out of the repetition of the storyline, even if it is already running in your head. Be aware though that caution is needed here, because I'm not saying that you must put all thoughts of this issue out of your head. Attempting to suppress a thought does not work very well and is likely to lead to it occurring more often. What you need to be able to do is to acknowledge silently and quickly the presence of the memory, but not to move on to the retelling. So you don't rerun the scenes, you don't create new lines of dialogue and you don't endlessly try to make it turn out right in fantasy. You acknowledge its reality and you leave it at that. When you take this approach resentment is able, gradually, to fade away to allow you to make the best of your life today.

◯ IN A NUTSHELL: Notice your resentments as they arise, but don't retell yourself the story for the umpteenth time—instead notice physical sensations (which will die away) and return your awareness to what you're doing.

WELL-WISHING

This is a version of an old mindfulness meditation called "Loving Kindness" that can be pleasantly beneficial if used often enough. It need only take a few minutes and here's how it goes:

Imagine that a friend or somebody else you love or admire is sitting in front of you, facing you. Try to sense a feeling of goodwill and well-wishing toward this person—allow yourself to really experience that feeling. Imagine yourself saying to them, "May you be happy. May you be well." Remind yourself that, like you, this person wants to have happy experiences and, like you, this person also has unhappy experiences. May you be happy. May you be well.

After a few moments this person is replaced by somebody else. That somebody else is yourself. Try to imagine looking at yourself sitting in front of you. Try to sense for yourself that same feeling of goodwill and well-wishing that you had toward the person you love or admire. Wish yourself well.

A third person comes and sits in front of you. This is somebody toward whom your feelings are negative. In deciding who that person will be for this exercise, you don't have to pick your worst enemy; just choose somebody toward whom you have some negativity or whom you judge somewhat unfavorably. Looking at that person, see if you can feel that sense of goodwill and well-wishing toward them. Then silently wish them well. If you find it too difficult to wish this person well, redirect the well-wishing toward yourself instead.

This practice is beneficial to you in many ways. For example, while you are wishing well to these other people, you step outside the victim role. Even if you feel overwhelmed by external forces, these few minutes of well-wishing take you out of that state as you wish others well. Try it a few times and see if you like it.

By the way, you can also choose to visualize just one person for this practice. I once did it only with somebody who had annoyed me, but with whom I also wanted to do business. It helped me to clear my mind of resentment and focus on the matter at hand, with rewarding results.

◌ IN A NUTSHELL: The well-wishing meditation takes you out of victim mode and into giving mode and can boost your sense of well-being. If you only have time to visualize one person, that's fine too.

In summary: In this chapter we have looked at the many ways in which mindfulness can improve our relationships with other people and with ourselves. In particular, it helps us to step out of habitual ways of seeing and interacting with other people and it can help us to avoid becoming mired in resentments as time goes on.

WHAT QUALITY
AM I BRINGING?

Practice: Now and then, pause and ask yourself: What quality am I bringing to this moment?

Commentary: The beauty of asking this question is that you don't have to answer it. Asking the question takes you out of the swirl of events and emotions for a moment. In that moment, you come into awareness, you notice how you are reacting and you may choose to change your reaction. This is especially useful if your reaction is an old one, drawn from a past pattern of relating to people and events that may no longer serve you well.

If you want to go deeper: Pause further and ask yourself if you could take a more helpful or skillful attitude. No need to sit around analyzing. If a better alternative is available, it will probably suggest itself fairly quickly.

CHECK IN WITH YOUR EXPERIENCE

Practice: Pause and notice your breathing. Now notice your posture—how you are sitting, standing, walking, running or lying down. Next, notice the sounds in your environment. Now, your breathing again.

Commentary: Mindfulness is often described as being "in the now." But the "now" can be an abstract idea, and by the time you realize you're in the now it's probably gone! It's more useful to think of mindfulness as paying attention to what your senses are bringing you. This simple practice does that and can take less than a minute; though, if you prefer, you can do it for many minutes. As you go through the practice, remember the key mindfulness instruction: Every time your mind drifts into thoughts, bring it back to what you're doing.

If you want to go deeper: As well as noticing your breathing, posture and sounds, notice also the feeling of your clothes against your body, your feet against the soles of your shoes and what your hands are doing. Don't worry about getting the order "right" or leaving something out.

FORM THE INTENTION

Practice: Form the intention to be mindful for the rest of your day.

Commentary: Mindfulness is intentional. You don't drift into mindfulness or awareness. You will find that the more you practice mindfulness, the more often you will be mindful. What you will be doing, though, is deliberately switching into mindfulness again and again. The more you practice mindfulness, the more quickly you will make that switch. Making the switch is the same as forming the intention to be mindful every time you notice you have been caught up in memories, fantasies or emotions. Whenever you form the intention to be mindful, this in itself takes you into the mindfulness zone.

If you want to go deeper: As you get up in the morning, form the intention to be mindful during the day. Renew the intention a couple of times as the day goes by. If you are going to a meeting or into a social situation, say silently, "I will be mindful during this."

LABEL THINKING
AS "THINKING"

Practice: Whenever you notice your mind has wandered off into memories, images, talking to itself and so on, label this silently with the word "thinking." Then return to your breathing or to whatever else you are doing.

Commentary: Labeling your thoughts (whatever they might be about) as "thinking" can help you to stop recycling resentments, fears and unhelpful scenes and to live instead in the reality of today. Labeling also helps if you want to spend some time focusing on your breath or on a task. Neuroscientists have found that labeling negative emotions helps to cool these emotions down, and meditators have been using this method for centuries.

If you want to go deeper: Use a more precise labeling system such as "angry," "anxious," "restless." Practice this technique by sitting still for a couple of minutes and using that time to label thoughts and emotions that appear in your mind.

WHAT IS MY MIND
TELLING ME?

Practice: Ask, every now and then, "What is my mind telling me about this?"

Commentary: The "this" could be your day, a person, an issue, a project, the weather—anything, in other words. When you ask the question, the answer that comes instantly can be surprising. You may find that your mind exaggerates situations, grumbles unnecessarily or is replaying old ideas you thought you had left behind. Ask the question and learn something about the patterns of thinking that drive you.

If you want to go deeper: After asking the question, pause. Consider whether the contents of your mind include old thoughts from old situations that no longer apply. Ask yourself what a more useful thought might be.

10

MINDFULNESS AT WORK

If major corporations provide mindfulness sessions for their staff, it's a safe bet that mindfulness is good for business. But the employees enjoy mindfulness practice because it's good for them too. So whether you work for someone else or you run your own business, this chapter is for you. If you start practicing mindfulness, even in a small but consistent way, you'll soon see the benefits—it will boost your capacity to keep a clear head, make a space for creativity and help you to handle yourself well in meetings and to plan realistically. Let's begin with keeping a cool head in the workplace.

KEEPING YOUR COOL UNDER PRESSURE

For most of us, pressures come with the workplace territory, whether that territory is a corner shop, a large corporation or a classroom. The pressures we most readily identify come from the outside—the over-demanding boss, the escalating workload, delays in getting supplies and so on. However, the pressures mindfulness practice can best help us with are those that come from within ourselves. We all work from unexamined assumptions that make our working lives more difficult than they need to be. These can include the assumption that you must never say "No," that you must meet each and every demand and that you must be more impressive than anybody else. But when you practice a little mindfulness every day you get better at spotting these assumptions and stepping back from them—that is, stepping out of autopilot. You need to do this because it's operating on autopilot that leads you to say "yes" when you ought to say "no," and that scrunches you into a ball of stress without you even realizing it. Autopilot can rule, and ruin, your working life.

To counteract the autopilot tendency, use the mindfulness techniques elsewhere in this book, especially in Chapters 3 and 4, because an awareness of your posture and your breath will help enormously, as will asking questions like "What is my mind telling me?" (see p. 145) or "What quality am I bringing?" (see p. 141).

When it comes to external pressures, make sure you distinguish between those that are truly external and those that actually come from within yourself. For example, is the demand that you finish this huge task by the weekend being imposed on you by yourself or is it coming from your boss or customers? What's stopping you from asking for an extension—you or them? A mindful pause can help you to spot your motives for reacting the way you do, to see the choices that are open to you and to make better ones.

○ IN A NUTSHELL: Practice mindfulness to help you to *choose* responses, rather than acting blindly out of unexamined assumptions.

A SPACE FOR CREATIVITY

Your mind is a creative space. Look at what you can conjure up in your imagination. Look at your fantasies. Look at how vivid a dream can be during the night when you're sleeping. Look at the good ideas that "just came" to you when you least expected it.

So why does all that creativity get pushed aside in the workplace? It's because when you go round and round in the same patterns of thinking and reacting day after day, your creativity is stifled; it doesn't go away, but it's very hard for ideas to get through the noise in your conscious mind. To take an example I've already mentioned, imagine a child in a roomful of adults loudly discussing a problem. The child knows the answer, but the adult chatter drowns out her voice. And that's how it can be with creative ideas.

The practice of mindfulness clears a space for the fruits of your creativity to come to the surface. Have you ever allowed yourself to relax really deeply on holiday? If so, you'll probably have noticed how the absence of clutter in your head allows creativity to flourish. Good, creative ideas—even life-changing ones—about your present work or your future direction emerge into your awareness by the pool.

It's a bit like the phrase "sleep on it," which is really a plea to allow your mind to work on a problem without interference from you—in other words, to allow your creative system to do its job. Great literature, great paintings, great movies—none of these come about through an intensive application of logical thought. They emerge. And it is only after they emerge that they then require the application of logical judgment and refining—once the chicken has hatched. But the chicken will never be hatched if the hen is too busy dashing around to sit on the egg.

○ IN A NUTSHELL: If you do creative work, practice mindfulness to clear a space into which ideas can emerge.

AND NOBODY HAS TO KNOW!

The great thing about practicing mindfulness is that you don't have to sit on your desk in the lotus position. Nobody has to know you're being mindful unless you want to tell them. Of course, if you are Extremely Important, you can announce to your minions that you are off to meditate and must not be disturbed. But as most of us are not Extremely Important, read on for some ways to practice mindfulness unobtrusively:

- As you sit at your desk, breathe out with awareness occasionally. Resist the temptation to micromanage your breathing: think of your breath as falling gently out of your body as you observe.

- Become aware of your posture. See if you can do your work without scrunching up your shoulders and neck muscles.

- When you move around the workplace, bring your awareness to your walking.

- Have you got a picture on the wall in your office? When's the last time you really saw it?

- Bring a little mindfulness to your work on the computer and the multiplicity of other gadgets in your world. For instance, make a practice of entering passwords mindfully instead of stabbing the screen or the keyboard and swearing when it doesn't work. Look up from the screen sometimes and notice yourself breathing. Notice your fingers touching the keyboard.

- Notice yourself breathing when you pick up the phone, or notice yourself picking up the phone. Connect with your breath during the phone call. If you're texting, check in with your awareness that you're texting.

○ IN A NUTSHELL: Practice mindfulness at your desk, when walking around your workplace, when entering passwords or using the phone—these are all opportunities to become more mindful discreetly.

MINDFULNESS IN MEETINGS

A meeting is never just a meeting. For some it's an exercise in power. For others it's an opportunity to demonstrate that they belong. Some conduct meetings as though they are in the schoolyard, others as if they are engaging in a polite ritual. With all this, and more, going on, the benefits of keeping a clear head through staying mindful are great. You will be less likely to get yourself talked into something that you shouldn't be getting talked into; and you will be more likely to pause for thought when you are under pressure.

Good manipulators may try to lead you in a direction that suits them by outmaneuvering, undermining, flattery, the presentation of half facts and other tricks. It pays to be alert to these undercurrents. But how? Keep 10 percent of your awareness on your breath or your posture (either will do) and you will be more likely to notice them.

If you're nervous about meetings, a little mindfulness practice beforehand will help. Try the 7/11 technique—breathe in to a count of seven and out to a count of eleven.

◯ IN A NUTSHELL: Dip into awareness of your breathing at meetings to give yourself a perspective on what is going on.

MINDFUL PLANNING

Mindfulness isn't a matter of drifting along aimlessly in a boat called "now." People in busy jobs sometimes worry about this, asking: "How can I plan if I'm in the now? Isn't everything going to fall apart?"

Not at all. Planning belongs to the now, not to the future. Once you understand that—by recognizing the difference between planning, reminiscence and fantasy—you can apply mindfulness with beneficial results. So let's suppose your job is to arrange the facilities for the annual conference of your company. Last year you discovered too late that the hotel parking facilities were more than a mile from the hotel and guests had to trudge all the way back to the hotel after parking. Purple faces and pursed lips all around. If, when you get to work on this year's conference, you say, "Right, that was a horrible experience. Never again. This time I'll double-check that the hotel has on-site parking," that's mindful planning; but if, instead, you sit replaying the whole horrible event blow by blow in your mind, that's reminiscing. Respecting the difference between the two can make a major difference both to the effectiveness of your planning and to your ability to plan without stressing yourself out.

The same goes for fantasy. You've booked a hotel on the side of a cliff overlooking the Atlantic because you think it will make an unusual and interesting venue. But your imagination wonders: What if global warming has caused the cliff to erode? What if the hotel spins off into the ocean with your customers inside it, as you stand on the edge haplessly looking on? That's not planning, that's fantasy. Arranging a visit to the hotel, complete with a sneaky look over the side to check that the cliff is still standing—that's planning.

Try this: Jot down your main tasks for next week. Consider when you might do them or what the order of priority might be. Every time your mind runs off into reminiscence or fantasy, gently but firmly bring it back to planning. Develop that mindfulness-planning muscle and it will keep you in good stead both at work and in your home life.

◯ IN A NUTSHELL: To plan mindfully, keep bringing your attention back to the task when it drifts off into reminiscence or fantasy.

In summary: Mindfulness will help you to keep a cool head in the workplace. Interactions with others, creativity, planning and many other aspects of work will benefit. You can practice mindfulness in the workplace without interfering with your work and without anyone even knowing you are doing it. You will also find that the benefits of mindfulness will spread out into your social life.

MINDFULNESS AT THE DESK

The practice: If you are sitting at your desk, pause for a few moments and take in the sights and sounds around you, but without giving greater importance to one over the other.

Commentary: This pause will give you an opportunity to notice any tension in your body and to relax it. Are you working on a problem for which you need to generate some creative ideas? If so, the solution that was (hopefully) waiting in your subconscious all the time will now get a chance to come through and be heard. The pause also gives you a chance to step out of the racing of your thoughts. If you have a habit of working too late in the evening, the pause may give you the space in which to notice that it is way after finishing time. Time to think of going home!

If you want to go deeper: As you pause and look around, bring your awareness to your body in the chair, to your posture and to your breathing. Notice your feet against the floor. All of this helps to improve your presence of mind in work situations.

11

MINDFULNESS AND EMOTIONAL DISTRESS

Isn't it odd that we don't like to talk about anxiety or depression, yet both are universal human experiences? Fortunately, mindfulness practice can help us with both of these conditions, and can do so whether or not we share with other people the fact that they affect us. Let's begin by looking at anxiety, including panic attacks, and then at the ways in which mindfulness can help with depression, especially in protecting against relapse. We will also consider issues around grief and loss, as well as bullying.

ANXIETY

As you are probably aware, anxiety has a mental, emotional and physical side, each of which is all too obvious when we are in its grip: thoughts about what will happen (or not happen) in the future go round and round in our minds; emotionally, we feel fearful; physically, we are tensed up or may even feel sick. But mindfulness can help—because with a mindful approach to anxiety, we accept the emotional and physical feelings and we decide that we will not get caught up in the scary stories our mind wants to tell us about the future. So let's suppose that at 9 o'clock on Monday morning you have a meeting with your doctor about the outcome of an important medical test; it's a safe bet that the appointment will be on your mind for the weekend. If you indulge your thoughts about it, you will see no end to the catastrophes your mind can make up. But in mindfulness you acknowledge the existence of the fearful thoughts, then focus your attention on how that feels in your body. So you may have a dart of fear about Monday morning in your chest, but you don't follow the story about it in your mind. You just think about the physical feeling, acknowledge it and move on. Your mind can create worries without end, but physical feelings rise and fall. That's why it's far more helpful to put your attention on how you feel your anxiety physically, rather than dwelling on thoughts about the emotion.

As I said earlier, this is not about switching off your emotions. What I am talking about here is developing the ability to tolerate your own uncomfortable feelings. People who are unable to tolerate their feelings of discomfort find their lives restricted by that fact. For instance, if you cannot bear the idea of flying, you have to rule out many destinations for holidays or work and you may miss important family events abroad. But if you learn to acknowledge and endure the fear, you move out of paralysis. The ability to tolerate your own feelings of discomfort is hugely important. Indeed, it's liberating. If a fear is very deep or extreme, additional therapy may be needed, but this will almost always involve some degree of mindful toleration. For many of our everyday feelings of discomfort or nervousness, however, mindfulness alone will be sufficient.

(**Note**: Of course, I'm not suggesting here that you ignore a warning voice if it seems you are about to do something unwise or dangerous.)

○ IN A NUTSHELL: **If you can do something helpful about issues** that cause you anxiety, do it. If you can't do anything about them, avoid the habit of repeating negative thoughts and scary scenarios in your mind. Such thinking makes matters worse. Instead, bring your attention to your breathing, to your physical sensations or to whatever you are meant to be doing at the moment.

Panic attacks. A panic attack can include shortness of breath, pounding heartbeat, sweating, the fear of falling, nausea and other symptoms. Panic attacks can occur in many places: a shopping center, the office, a busy street, even your own home. They are often irrational and impossible to predict. And they are very unpleasant. If you have ever had a panic attack, you will know—especially if you have had a series of them—that the main harm they do is limit freedom of movement. This limitation comes as the sufferer tries to avoid situations in which the feared panic attack might occur. A typical scenario for a person experiencing panic attacks is that when they suddenly notice the first signs coming on they begin to tell themselves how terrible it is that they are having the attack. They also tell themselves that they need to get out of the situation they are in, so as to bring the panic attack to a close as quickly as possible. What this means, though, is that the panic attack is now dictating their behavior. A mindfulness perspective, on the other hand, suggests that it is better to be able to endure the panic attack and not to have to run away from it into another situation: The way to deal with it is to accept it.

Your panic attack may not have a cause in external reality. It may be due to a spike in anxiety or even to a change in carbon dioxide levels in your bloodstream, which, in itself, may be a very temporary event. Try the following strategies to deal with your panic attack effectively:

- Decide that instead of trying to get away from it, you will observe the panic attack as it rises and falls (this could take about twenty minutes).

- Instead of saying, "This is awful," etc., try saying something like "This is unpleasant, but it's not the end of the world." Alternatively, you could use a traditional phrase like "This too will pass."

- Try to breathe in a reasonably normal fashion, as gulping air can make matters worse.

- Remember that in all likelihood nobody else knows you are having a panic attack.

◌ IN A NUTSHELL: Learning to tolerate panic attacks as they rise and fall can give you greater control over where you go and what you do.

DEPRESSION

Because this is a condition many of us are afraid to talk about, we can spend too much time in our own heads, thinking about the causes of our depression. That's a problem in itself because rumination, or brooding on your troubles, is linked to depression. In other words, our response to depression sometimes makes it worse.

When events happen that are deeply upsetting, we can fall into depression, especially if they involve loss—such as the loss of a person, status or a home. And to a certain extent that's natural. What can be disabling, though, is the recurrence of depression. People who have had three or more bouts are at a very high risk of suffering another within a year.

Fortunately, mindfulness has a great deal to offer those caught in this vicious circle through the pioneering work of Professor Mark Williams of Oxford University. What Williams has found is that the practice of mindfulness when you are not depressed can offer substantial protections against relapse. He has developed a mindfulness-based cognitive-behavioral therapy course that has reduced relapse rates by 50 percent or more. That's a great result and it has been replicated in many studies. While this course involves attendance at weekly sessions for a period, the results suggest that the practice of mindfulness in itself, in the ways described in this book, is beneficial if you suffer from depression.

So if you can find a mindfulness group near you, consider joining them in practicing this very valuable skill, but if not, use the book and the many mindfulness resources you can find on the internet. (For instance, you can find many of Professor Williams's mindfulness presentations on YouTube. You can also subscribe, at no cost, to my newsletter and daily mindfulness emails through my website, www.padraigomorain.com.)

So remember the key point here: Practice mindfulness when you are not depressed in order to gain the benefits. If you do so, you are far less likely to ruminate on your troubles and more likely to be active, and both can help protect against depression.

⟲ IN A NUTSHELL: Practice mindfulness between bouts of depression to reduce the risk of relapse.

GRIEF AND LOSS

Mindfulness doesn't take grief away. But a point comes when the full flood of grieving is ready to abate enough to allow a reengagement with daily living. And that is when mindfulness practice can be particularly helpful.

Mindfulness can enable you to honor the pain of your loss while maintaining a fresh awareness of what the present has to offer. You may need to give yourself permission to reengage with the present. This is because people who grieve can feel guilty about enjoying life again. Then, having given yourself permission to reengage, you need to notice what is happening in the here and now.

Moreover, mindfulness practice will, when you are ready, help you to cease ruminating about your loss and this will have the important effect of helping you to avoid slipping from grief into depression.

When practicing mindfulness, you are encouraged to return again and again to an awareness of whatever is going on right now. That may be your breathing, sounds you hear, what you see, what you are doing with your hands or your walking. It is in returning from rumination to awareness that you begin to find peace again.

With the practice of mindfulness you give yourself permission to reconnect with the world and with the joy that can still visit you in your own life, perhaps when you least expect it.

○ IN A NUTSHELL: When you have grieved for a time, allow yourself to expand your awareness to include the external world. Let your loss become part of your experience and not your whole experience.

WORKPLACE/SCHOOL BULLYING

Emotionally, bullying does harm in three ways: through anticipation, through the event itself and through the aftermath. The anticipation of being bullied can make it impossible for the target to work to his or her best standard, to sleep or even to eat. During the event itself, the bullied person is stressed and afraid. Spending the rest of the day going over and over what happened means no rest, little energy for a social life and perhaps a reliance on drink or drugs.

Advice on an overall approach to bullying is outside the scope of this book, but mindfulness practice can help in this distressing situation. By returning mindfully again and again to your present-moment experience, the frequency with which your emotions are hijacked by the anticipation and the aftermath will be reduced. Try a little 7/11 breathing (see p. 32) or do some mindful walking (see p. 53). What is important here is returning your attention from the scenes of bullying to your breathing, walking and other activities.

Keeping some of your attention on your breathing while the bullying is going on can help you to maintain presence of mind during the event. If you plan to use some assertiveness skills with the bully, you need to maintain enough presence of mind to use these approaches, and mindfulness of breathing can help you to cultivate that. (Appropriate assertiveness skills depend on the situation, but examples are saying things like "I would prefer if you did not shout at me in public," or "What exactly is it that gives you the right to speak to me like that?"). Sometimes bullies are baffled and drop their obnoxious behavior when the target displays presence of mind and stays out of the victim role.

Cyberbullying (which happens to adults as well as to school-children) plays havoc with the emotions of the person on the receiving end. Mindfulness practice can help cool down the emotions and make the target less prone to having their emotions hijacked by taunts (though these will still hurt). All this, in turn, will give him or her enough clarity of mind to be able to see choices. These could include blocking the bullies, taking a calming breath before opening a text or limiting their own time on social media until the bullies get bored and move on.

◯ IN A NUTSHELL: Practice mindfulness instead of recycling remembered scenes of bullying in your mind.

In summary: Mindfulness practice can make a huge contribution to how you deal with emotional distress, and by using it you will gradually notice the benefits in your own life. Mindfulness doesn't always make the sources of emotional distress go away, but it changes your relationship to that distress, so that you are no longer overwhelmed by it.

MOOD SURFING

Practice: Notice your mood and observe it without getting caught up in thoughts about it.

Commentary: Moods come and go like clouds in the sky. Analyzing where a mood has come from and why is usually a waste of time: better to spend your energy on whatever it is that you need to do next. Thinking about a negative mood can drag you further into it. If you get on with whatever else you need to do, the mood will eventually fade by itself.

If you want to go deeper: Look at a photograph of somebody who means a lot to you and observe the mood that arises without repeating to yourself the story about the person or the relationship.

MAKE SPACE FOR LITTLE HAPPINESSES

Practice: Decide to appreciate the small happinesses in your life by being mindful of them as they happen.

Commentary: The British philanthropist Thomas Horsfall said that "the greatest happiness Man can have is to have a great many little happinesses." Most of us experience little happinesses, even when life is failing to deliver on the big-ticket items. Morning sunlight on the trees, a piece of music on the radio, a momentary sense of ease—all are little happinesses, and it is greatly to our loss if we allow them to pass by unnoticed. As you practice mindfulness, you will begin to notice and be enriched by them.

If you want to go deeper: Spend some time deliberately noticing the "small happinesses" around you: the beautiful designs on household items, the harmony in certain spaces, for instance. Make a practice out of bringing them to your attention frequently, knowing that they won't be with you forever.

FEEL GOOD FOR LONGER

Practice: Next time you catch yourself feeling good, connect with that feeling for a while.

Commentary: This counteracts our tendency to take good feelings for granted, while paying attention to "bad" feelings. Notice that good feeling, noting where it is located in your body. Now and then check back for it. No need to cling to it—your feeling will inevitably change—nor should you analyze it to pieces; simply be alive to it and aware of it while you have it.

If you want to go deeper: Observe the nature of the feeling. Does it have an energy? If you breathe in to the feeling, what's that like? Can you think of an image to represent the feeling? Note that this is different from intellectual analyzing—instead it is a way of "being with" the feeling.

12

A MONTH OF MINDFULNESS

The calendar that follows provides a quick and easy way to remind yourself to practice mindfulness every day. Simply look for the day of the month (1 to 31) and try out the practice you find under that date. Use the calendar for a while and you will notice yourself becoming more mindful, with associated benefits for your well-being and stress levels.

1

Breathe for the moment. Your breathing is neither in the past nor in the future. It is now. Every time you become aware of your breathing you connect with mindfulness in the moment.

2

At least three times today, pause and do a quick body scan. Become aware of your body, moving your awareness from the top of your head to your toes. After you have completed the quick body scan, remain at rest for a few moments. During those few moments, become aware of your body breathing.

3

Set your timer: Come into mindfulness when an hour has passed. This is an easy way to remember to be mindful. Whenever you realize an hour has passed, bring your attention for a little while to whatever is going on right now. Do this, for instance, by noticing your breathing, your posture or sounds in your environment.

4

Pause, now and then, and ask yourself: "What is my mind telling me about this?" When you ask the question the answer that comes instantly can be surprising. You may find that your mind exaggerates situations, grumbles unnecessarily or is replaying old ideas you thought you had left behind. When you realize this, you can step outside it and make better choices.

5

Put a few moments aside to become aware of the pause at the end of your out-breath. To notice this tiny pause you need to be still and paying attention. Experience it without trying to manage or lengthen it. Then observe it being followed, quite effortlessly, by the in-breath.

6

Remember that your happiness probably does not depend on whatever you are worrying about right now. When you find yourself feeling anxious or upset at some everyday situation, remind yourself that your happiness does not depend on this. You will probably have forgotten the situation by this time next week. Say silently "My happiness does not depend on this."

7

Slightly slow down some of your actions today. You can slow down many actions just a little without anyone noticing. This will help you to maintain mindfulness while you are doing them. Common actions you could choose include washing your hands, opening doors and entering passwords.

8

Be aware as you stand up or sit down. We often stand or sit without any awareness of what we are doing. Bringing awareness to this simple act will take you into the present moment many times a day. The effects will continue well beyond the moments involved in standing or sitting.

9

Bring your attention to your shoulders now and then and allow them to relax. We tense up our shoulders unconsciously. This is especially the case when we are driving, hurrying or concentrating. Noticing our shoulders brings us into mindfulness and reduces physical tension.

10

Recognize the golden moment in mindfulness practice. Mindfulness practice has a golden moment: It's the moment you realize your mind has drifted away. That's when you bring your attention back to your breath, to your body or to whatever you are doing. It's by constantly returning your attention that you strengthen your capacity for mindfulness in your daily life.

11

Drink your tea or coffee mindfully. When you are aware of your actions as you carry them out, you are being mindful. Today, try to remain aware that you are drinking a cup of tea, coffee or other beverage while you are drinking it. Not only will you be mindful but, as a bonus, you will get more enjoyment out of your drink.

12

Use awareness to pull your scattered mind together. Do you ever feel your mind is "all over the place"? Bringing your awareness to your breath will take you back into the moment. This works best if you focus on one particular place where you feel your breath, such as your nostrils.

13

Notice pleasurable moments. We have an extraordinary habit of discounting pleasurable moments to focus on our frustrations. Pause sometimes to become mindful of the small pleasures in your day. Don't let them slip by in forgetfulness.

14

When walking today, do so in awareness and without unnecessary hurry. When walking in our workplace or to the shops we often do so tensely, as if we are being pushed along under duress. Try walking along in a relaxed way with awareness of the sights and sounds around you. You can do this even if you need to walk quickly.

15

Choose a sense to which you will bring mindful awareness as often as you can today. Mindfulness usually involves our senses because it is difficult to be mindful in any other way. Give attention to one of your senses today, such as hearing, touch, smell or the kinesthetic (bodily movement) sense. Try choosing a sense to which you usually pay little attention.

16

Use awareness of posture as a quick and easy gateway to mindfulness. Now and then bring your awareness to the fact that you are standing, walking, sitting or lying down. This is a very good (and traditional) way to come into mindfulness and it's usually relaxing too. Remember, your body isn't in the past or the future—it's here, right now.

17

Practice the art of waiting mindfully. We get to do a lot of waiting, and instead of regarding it as "dead time" we can make use of it to aid our mindfulness practice. Notice opportunities to bring awareness to your breath or posture as you wait. Allow your mind to clear, if only for a few moments.

18

Pause and notice your breathing, now your posture, now sounds in your environment, now your breathing again. Practice doing a quick check-in like this now and then during your day. It doesn't take long and can take you straight out of a preoccupation with regrets or worries and into contact with the present moment. It can also give you a sense of presence of mind in the middle of a busy day.

19

Check what's happening with your body when you are sitting down. Without realizing it, you can slouch or tense yourself up when sitting at a desk or table. If you bring your awareness to your body from time to time, you will get better at noticing this. Awareness of the body can bring a valuable sense of presence of mind.

20

Choose a mindful space. Identify a space you find yourself in many times a day. This could be the kitchen, the bathroom or a coffee shop, for instance. Practice being mindful while you are in that space.

21

As you go through your day, ask yourself, "What is my intention?" Knowing your intention is an old and useful mindfulness practice. The alternative can be to drift rather aimlessly. Start with small, everyday matters—for example, "What did I come into this shop to buy?"

22

Use today's inconveniences to develop your mindfulness practice. When you are mindful, ordinary inconveniences and frustrations don't seem to matter as much. Try to cope mindfully with today's inconveniences, such as traffic, the needs of family or employers, late deliveries, disagreeable weather and so on. A practical tip is to avoid making speeches in your head about how terrible these inconveniences are.

23

If you detect a feeling of happiness, appreciate its presence without analyzing it to pieces. From time to time, if you pay attention, you will notice you are feeling happy. Because happiness comes and goes, you can improve the quality of your experience by remaining aware of it while it lasts, but without clinging to it.

24

Return to mindfulness when your imagination flares up and takes you away from the reality of the moment. Your reactions don't only include your response to whatever has just happened. They also include a flare-up of memories, thoughts and physical feelings. When you spot a flare-up, become mindful of your breath or body to make a space in which you can step back and see your choices.

25

Allow negative emotions to go in their own time. When you feel annoyance, frustration or anxiety, allow yourself to feel the physical sensation that goes with it. Stay out of any drama about it in your head. Allow time for the feeling to die away.

26

Return your attention now and then to your anchor point—the place where you are most aware of your breathing. You may be most aware of your breath in your nostrils, your throat, chest or tummy. Return your attention to this anchor point for a few moments when you are alone. At meetings, bring your attention back to your anchor point to gain some degree of detachment.

27

Whenever you eat today, do it mindfully. Use the many opportunities for mindful awareness that eating offers, and get more enjoyment out of your food at the same time. Notice taste, texture and aroma. Slow down your eating a little.

28

Give some attention today to what your hands are doing. When you wash your hands, notice the temperature of the water and the feel of the soap. Notice when you touch your face. Are your hands warm or cool right now?

29

Allow yourself to stop thinking about issues you cannot resolve. Like everybody else, you enter today with some issues from the near or distant past that will never be resolved. Drop any tendency to keep uselessly trying to resolve these issues in your mind. Instead, return your attention from thoughts of these issues to whatever else is going on in your experience right now, or to your breathing.

30

Intend to be mindful today. In the morning, afternoon and evening form the intention to be mindful. This, in itself, will bring you into the present moment. What normally happens at the start of each of these periods in your day that could remind you to form that intention?

31

When talking to or looking at another person, step out of the judgments and stories you usually repeat to yourself about them. Bring a sense of curiosity to your engagement with familiar people. Don't assume you know what they're thinking. Press pause and hold off, for a little while, on commenting on them in your mind.

13

TEN STRATEGIES FOR EVERYDAY MINDFULNESS

In this section, you will learn how to apply mindfulness to common situations in everyday life, find pockets of time for mindfulness that won't disrupt your day and learn about some quick mindfulness techniques.

1. OVERWHELMING DAYS

Ever had an overwhelming day? I have them too, but one day, when the list of items on my to-do list looked more overwhelming than usual, it struck me that the only way to maintain any peace of mind as I worked through it was to be very, very mindful. I learned to apply a mindfulness technique called "bare attention," and the "overwhelm" has been much reduced ever since.

"Bare attention" means looking at something without adding comments, fantasies or memories in your head, like: How am I supposed to get through all this? How much time must I spend on the phone to that call center?

By pulling your attention back from these thoughts, you get to conserve your energy for what you have to actually do, instead of wasting time "awfulizing," as some psychologists call it. So, for instance, instead of upsetting yourself by complaining in advance about the hassle involved in phoning the call center, you focus your energy on picking up the phone and making the call. The experience may still turn out to be as bad as you'd expected, but by practicing mindfulness you at least don't have to go through it three times (i.e., anticipating it, doing it and then complaining endlessly about it). Instead, you go through it just once.

Here are a couple of simple techniques I practice to increase my ability to use bare attention:

One-minute mindfulness. Set a timer on your laptop to count down one minute. Every hour or so, start the timer and hold your attention on your breathing, as best you can, for that minute (you will be surprised how quick the mind is to drift away, even in such a short space of time). When the minute is up, return to work. This will help keep your stress levels lower and will make you more effective.

Mindfulness plus. Write a plus sign on top of your to-do list to remind yourself not to add unhelpful thoughts or stories when trying to concentrate on your work. Whenever you spot that plus sign, bring your attention back to the task in hand.

Simple mindfulness practices like these rescue you from that loop of memories, feelings and worries, so that you can get back to the relatively simple task at hand.

One very busy colleague spent four years intending to come to one of my mindfulness courses, but could never find the time. When she did finally get to a workshop she had to leave for a couple of hours in the middle to go to a meeting. Nevertheless, when she applied the mindfulness approaches she had learned, her days became calmer and less stressed, even though she was still a very busy woman. Such is the value of mindfulness and bare attention in a demanding environment. This technique can work for you too.

2. DON'T LET TOMORROW SPOIL TODAY

Ignoring what's happening today while you fret about tomorrow is a universal human failing. If you're a person whose Sunday evenings are dominated by glum thoughts of Monday morning, you'll know what I mean. But this is not just about Sunday evenings; it's about our tendency to allow that unappetizing tomorrow to reach back and spoil today. Fortunately, mindfulness is the antidote.

For most of us, it's all too easy to fall into a sort of trance of thoughts about the future when we're walking in the park, strolling by the beach or relaxing at home. Then we go back to work unrefreshed because we were not there for our leisure activities.

Here are two techniques you can use to get your mind and your attention out of the future and into the present.

Give deliberate attention to the good times. Every night or every morning take a couple of minutes to recall some of the good things that happened to you during the day (or previous day). This will attune you to recognizing the positive. Unless you're very unlucky, every weekend, holiday and day is pleasant at least some of the time. Learn to recognize and acknowledge these times. Don't let them pass by in a flash while you give all your attention to your dissatisfactions.

Don't mope. Moping is a waste of the limited time we have on this earth. If it's Sunday evening and you're not keen on Monday mornings, go to a movie, walk with a friend, get down on the floor and play with your kids. And every time you think of the office, pull your attention back to whatever you're doing right here and now. This doesn't just apply to Sunday evenings, but to all those days we waste by living in the future.

Now, imagine you go on a bus trip in which you travel across spectacular mountains and through beautiful valleys, but you fall asleep and dream that you are back in the office. You wake up only when the journey ends. Wouldn't you feel cheated? Wouldn't you feel you had lost those hours from your life? Wouldn't you wish you had never set off on the journey? Mindfulness wakes you up during the trip.

To bring your attention back, notice:

- your breathing; this is your ever-present anchor to the here and now
- sounds in your immediate environment and outside it—birds, cars, music, voices, footsteps, for instance
- the feeling of your feet against the ground or floor while you walk
- the conversation you are having right now

The more you experience of the present, the more you experience of your life. Your life isn't happening in the past and it isn't happening in the future: It's happening right now.

A woman at one of my mindfulness workshops said that practicing mindfulness was like stretching out time. Life no longer passed her by like a dream: She was present for as much of it as she could be.

3. A MINDFUL DAY

When I began to practice mindfulness I found it was easy to forget it in a busy day. And with a succession of busy days mindfulness went out the door altogether—just when I needed it most. If you've been trying to practice mindfulness you may have found the same.

I looked for ways to make mindfulness part of my day. Essentially, I needed simple mindfulness opportunities throughout the day and evening—which is a lot easier than it sounds, as you will discover if you try it.

What I am suggesting is that you divide the day up into morning, daytime and evening and build mindfulness practices into those time slots in ways that are natural for you.
Try these approaches:

Morning—select one or two of these:

- Notice your breathing before getting up.

- Form the intention to be mindful.

- Move your attention out of your thoughts and on to your breathing or the feeling of your feet against the floor.

- Brush your teeth with awareness.

- Notice the lights switching on and the kettle starting to boil.

During the day—select one or two of these:

- Every now and then, pause and notice your breathing or posture.

- Bring awareness to switching on a computer or entering a password.

- When having lunch, notice that you are eating.

- Use 7/11 breathing a couple of times (see p. 32).

Evening—select one or two of these:

- On arriving home, switch your attention to the home.

- If working from home, take a minute to notice your breathing when you've finished work to bring your attention back to home life.

- When you go to bed, notice your out-breath for a while.

- When you wake up during the night, try a body scan (see p. 54) to help you sleep.

So for me, I like to form the intention to be mindful as soon as I get out of bed and to switch my attention to my breathing when I am in the kitchen.

During the day I make a point of entering passwords mindfully and I bring awareness to the experience of eating my lunch.

And in the evening, if I have been out, I switch my awareness from what is going on in my head to what is going on in the house as soon as I arrive home.

This method liberated a man who came to my mindfulness classes. He had tried to meditate mindfully for half an hour a day, but he couldn't do it—he had small kids who wanted his attention whenever he was home and he was reluctant to say no to them. Therefore, he regarded himself as a failure at meditation. I advised him to quit feeling bad about this "failure" and to build mindfulness unobtrusively into his day, as recommended above. He did so by, for instance, deliberately being mindful of his kids' chatter in the mornings and before long he was enjoying the benefits of mindfulness.

4. REPAIRING RELATIONSHIPS

Not all fractured relationships can be fixed and some hurts never heal. However, you can use mindfulness to allow hurts to die down and to develop a more objective perspective without denying the reality of what happened.

Here are two helpful approaches:

Move out of the story. Whenever you recall a hurtful memory, you feel a flash of distress. If you repeat to yourself the story behind that memory, you amplify that distress. Instead, quickly acknowledge the hurt while taking yourself out of the story. One way to do this is to return to awareness of your breath or of the activities around you. If the memory comes back often, use a word like "noted" when you feel the hurt and move on.

Use Naikan to balance relationships. This is a Japanese technique whereby you think of the person you are annoyed with—or anybody important to you in your life—and answer three questions.

- **What did I receive from this person?** Be specific. For instance, if the person is your mother, perhaps she got you dressed and out to school every morning, took you to the doctor when you were unwell, made dinner for you each evening and so on—be as specific as that.

- **What has this person received from me?** Again, be specific. You remembered her birthday, you helped her fix an electrical problem in the house, you took her on a holiday with your family, for example.

- **What difficulties have I caused this person?** Perhaps she had to give up work when you were born? Perhaps she had to be up out of bed earlier than she liked seven days a week when you were small to take care of you?

This exercise helps to balance the books, so to speak. Yes, you're angry with your mother, but she has, nonetheless, done many things for you and you have also done things for her. So you don't have to see her as all bad or all good and, although you created difficulties for her, you don't have to see yourself as all bad or all good either.

Emily worked with a colleague with whom she thought she had a close friendship and she was pleased when her friend was promoted. As her colleague moved up the ladder, though, she distanced herself from Emily and eventually shut down Emily's department, making Emily redundant. Emily suffered months of distress before trying the approaches above, having attended one of my workshops.

After a while, she still felt hurt but she no longer repeated the story endlessly in her mind. And when she did the Naikan exercise she realized that in the early days she'd had a genuine give-and-take relationship with her colleague. Gradually, Emily was able to cease dwelling on the hurt and to get herself back to emotional well-being. She still never wanted to speak to her former colleague again, but she no longer obsessed about what had happened. She had regained her autonomy and stability.

5. TEN POCKETS OF TIME

However busy you are, little pockets of time exist in your day. If you bring yourself back to mindfulness during these pockets of time, you will reduce your stress levels and gain presence of mind. Here are ten common time pockets.

1. **Bus stop, train station, traffic lights.** Quit fretting. Put your phone in your pocket. At a traffic light focus on your breathing, even if frustration has you all tensed up.

2. **Waiting for an elevator to arrive.** Instead of anxiously scanning the display to see what level the elevator is on, come into a sense of awareness, maybe noticing the sensation of your feet against the floor.

3. **Waiting for things to happen on your computer or phone.** You don't have to scrunch yourself up with frustration as wheels spin and egg timers turn on your screen. Use that time to become aware of your posture and to relax your shoulders.

4. **Sitting with a child.** Instead of trying to figure out work problems in your head when sitting with your children, try "being with" them for those

moments or minutes. Right now that's a great mindfulness exercise and in future you'll be glad you did it.

5. **Microwaving or making a sauce on the stove.** If something is going to take two whole minutes in the microwave or if a sauce is going to take three minutes to thicken, could you put your attention on it for that length of time? That way you'll practice mindfulness—and you won't burn the sauce.

6. **Waiting for water to get hot in the shower or from the tap.** Take this simple opportunity to pause and put your attention on to the changing temperature of the water.

7. **When a meeting ends.** Sit there for a few moments noticing your breathing while everyone else dives for their phones. Then gather up your stuff and check your emails if you need to.

8. **Waiting for the green man.** Are you someone who dashes across the street because the green man (in some cities, the green woman) is taking too long to appear on the pedestrian lights? If you are, try instead to look around in awareness while you wait for the light to change.

9. **Commercial breaks.** If you fast forward through the ads during breaks in TV shows, keep your attention on your breathing while you're doing so. If you don't fast forward, then keep bringing your attention back to your breath or your posture as you enjoy or endure the commercial break.

10. **Whenever you walk anywhere.** Going from one room to another, across the room, along a corridor, to the shop, up the stairs, to the parking lot,

you have an opportunity to bring your attention to your walking, noticing the feel of your feet against the ground or floor.

Make use of these time pockets and you will find you can be far more mindful in your day and your life without actually losing time.

A very stressed-out woman who was exhausted by combining motherhood with work outside the home came to me reluctantly (because meeting me meant skipping lunch) at the urging of her best friend. Her friend believed she could use mindfulness to lower her stress. She gave me half an hour of her time. I took out my list of mindfulness opportunities (similar to the one above), did a couple of brief mindfulness practices with her and asked her to identify opportunities for using those practices. When she came back to see me I could tell at once that her stress levels had fallen. As was her nature, she had worked diligently on her mindfulness practices and had even found longer periods of time in which to do them. Her children, her colleagues and her best friend all remarked on the positive change in her.

6. THE STRUGGLE SWITCH

It's Friday afternoon. You had hoped to hear the result of that interview for team leader. You call HR, but the manager has taken a long weekend and won't be back until Tuesday. You thump your desk. You bang the door on the way out. On the road home you get stuck in a traffic jam. You swear. You clench your fists.

Your struggle switch is on, even though your swearing and banging won't bring the HR manager back a moment sooner. Nor will it clear the traffic.

The struggle switch is a concept from a mindfulness-based approach called Acceptance and Commitment Therapy. Imagine you have a switch in your brain: when it's on, you struggle with reality, even if it's pointless to do so.

Most of us go around with the struggle switch on most of the time. If, say, you've spent years nagging a partner or child with absolutely no result, your struggle switch is probably stuck in the "on" position: the nagging makes no difference, but you do it anyway. If you've been getting angry at five o'clock every Monday morning for years because the garbage truck wakes you up, your struggle switch is stuck in the "on" position in relation to that situation.

Here are two approaches I use to avoid struggling pointlessly against reality and to keep my energy for when it *can* make a difference:

Flicking off the struggle switch when it doesn't help. Learn to spot the situations in which struggling is pointless: the rain falls when you wanted sunshine, your boss has had yet another silly idea that you are going to have to implement, your teenager will not clean up his or her catastrophic bedroom. In all these cases, reminding yourself to turn off the struggle switch will spare you useless emotional turmoil.

Distinguishing between "doing" mode and "being" mode. "Doing" mode is really good for practical problems—figuring out whether it makes more sense to go to a meeting by train or plane, or how to save money on your electricity bill, for instance. For other issues "doing" mode doesn't really work: Figuring out how to get rid of a sense of sadness at a recent loss is a prime example. In this case, you need to allow the sadness to take its course and pass in its own time. That "allowing" can be described as "being" mode.

Life—even your day—is full of issues you can do something about. Wasting energy on the ones you can't change is, well, a waste of energy. People who practice mindfulness don't waste energy if they can help it. They learn to flick off that struggle switch if it's pointless and they figure out when to use "doing" mode and when to use "being" mode, thereby becoming calmer in themselves and more effective at what they do.

Margaret, a very tidy person, had spent two years fighting with her teenage daughter about the state of the latter's bedroom. Her complaints fell on deaf ears and the issue caused many quarrels between them. When she heard about the struggle switch at one of my workshops, she decided to drop the pointless battle with her daughter and to ignore the existence of the bedroom. The atmosphere between them immediately improved and her daughter gradually grew into adulthood and became a very tidy mini-Margaret.

7. DROPPING RUMINATION

To ruminate is to brood, which means following a long chain of thoughts about a situation or person you dislike (we seem to ruminate on the negative, rather than the positive). If you've been a ruminator—and I was until I discovered mindfulness—you will know three things about rumination: it can be seductive, especially when the thoughts are about "poor me"; it can lead you gradually into a distressed or dark mood that's hard to get out of; and it achieves nothing in the real world.

I recall working with a man who brooded on the inadequacies of governments, organizations, bosses and colleagues. This man was actually good at what he did and a diligent worker, yet by indulging continually in rumination, he sentenced himself to a lifetime of useless anger. Another man, an alcoholic, went through periods of giving up drinking but, when sober, he could spend hours and hours ruminating on what he had missed out on in life because of drinking. This had the inevitable effect of sending him back to alcohol, with disastrous results.

If rumination plays too big a part in your day, here are two techniques I use and have found valuable:

Use a phrase like "moving on" to bring you back into contact with this moment's reality. Suppose you find yourself following a train of thought about a mistake you made some years ago. Once you spot what you are doing, say silently "moving on" and get back to awareness of your posture, your breathing or to whatever it is you ought to be doing right now. So, you don't try to resolve the issue you were ruminating about—because rumination rarely resolves anything; your aim is to let it alone for now by dropping that chain of thought. "Moving on" is a phrase I like to use, but if something else works better for you, then by all means use it.

Note your state of mind. Let's draw a quick distinction between your *state* of mind and the *contents* of your mind. If you are angry, then your state of mind is "angry." If you are angry because of a hurtful comment by your ex-partner, then your mind could be said to "contain" that comment. (Here is an everyday analogy: The water in the saucepan is boiling—that's the state of the water; the water is boiling an egg—that's the content of the water.) If you are given to rumination, one useful antidote is to note the state of your mind—"brooding mind," for instance. Simply noticing your state of mind will help to pull you out of rumination fairly quickly.

One woman who learned to drop the habit of rumination told me she felt as though a whole world had opened up to her. Suddenly, she was seeing people and places that had been invisible from behind the veil of rumination. She lost nothing when she gave up brooding, but she gained the excitement of engaging with the real, sometimes beautiful, world.

8. THE SAVING PAUSE

"If only I had kept my big mouth shut." Ever said that? Me too. A sharp, unthinking response to a partner or work colleague can require a lot of repair work. Or, at the other end of the spectrum is that too-quick agreement to do something that is actually someone else's job to do or that quick "yes" when the waiter asks you if everything was all right when, actually, everything was not all right.

A mindful pause can make a big difference in these and many other situations. In that pause you get a chance to think to yourself, "I need to say this" or "I had best not say that." Also, if you get into the habit of pausing for just a second or two before responding to other people, this will carry over into general decisionmaking.

A mindful pause gives you a second or two to see that you have more than one choice and to make the choice that is most likely to work. One participant in one of my workshops objected that a second or two isn't very much. "Think," I said, "of how many things you have done without a second's pause and that you would gladly go back and undo if you could." She didn't need long to think about it before she agreed that, yes, she could recall situations in which one or two seconds might have saved the day.

But how do you cultivate the ability to pause? Try these two techniques:

Pause for one in-breath or one out-breath before responding to another person in situations that are not emotionally charged. The more you practice like this, the more likely you are to pause mindfully when emotions are running high. (And a single in-breath or out-breath in the middle of a conversation is short and unobtrusive, so nobody even has to know you are using a technique.) So don't wait to use the pause until you are in the middle of a heated argument with somebody—that's like not learning to drive until the morning of the driving test.

Practice looking twice at everyday objects in your environment. We usually glance at such objects and move on instantly without noticing them. Looking twice means you have to pause. Again, this will give you the habit of pausing in the middle of situations in your day and that, in turn, will buy you time to make (hopefully) better choices or even to realize that you don't actually have to do anything.

John would rush to defend himself whenever anybody in his family voiced what he took to be a criticism. As he began to practice mindfulness, however, he slowly realized that not everything against which he defended himself was, in fact, criticism. Sometimes, he learned, he was misinterpreting a tone of voice or a simple observation. By teaching himself to pause for just one breath before responding, he stopped reacting to nonexistent attacks, and his relationships improved.

9. GOING AROUND IN CIRCLES

We are all prone to getting ourselves caught in reactions that keep us going around in circles. Mindfulness can counteract that. Here's the sequence: Something happens that awakens memories, feelings, thoughts, fantasies and even physical sensations. We now react to these memories, etc. even though they may have little to do with what is actually going on right now. If we are mindful we can spot this happening and we can step back from it; if we are not mindful we are in danger of being carried along by our reactions almost as though we are in a trance.

Suppose you go for a walk in a beautiful park on a pleasant morning. All is well until you spot a former friend—whose bad behavior destroyed the friendship—walking some distance away from you. What's likely to fill your mind now? Memories of your former friend's bad behavior and thoughts about what a rotten person this ex-friend is, all accompanied by physical tension and a raised heartbeat. You are going around in a very old and well-worn circle made up entirely of old reactions. Today, this ex-friend has done nothing to you and is not even aware of your presence in the park. What a waste of energy and of a good morning.

How do you stop yourself from going around in circles? Try these two techniques:

Pause the reaction. When you find yourself caught in a reaction, pause by noticing your breath and by suspending the self-talk that's going on in your head (such talk is normally part of such reactions). If you've been practicing mindfulness as part of your day you will find this much easier to do.

In the pause, consider that you probably have more than one choice and that one of these choices is to do nothing. One of the benefits of mindfulness is that it buys you a space in which to consider your choices. It also allows you to realize that non-action is sometimes preferable to action.

Amanda told me about going to her favorite restaurant on a Friday evening with her husband, Joe. They were about to order when Amanda's boss walked in. Immediately, Amanda recalled in vivid detail the argument they had earlier that day, which was just the latest in a series of quarrels.

It really annoyed her that her boss had sat herself down at a table in a restaurant where Amanda was trying to relax. How dare she? It was just too much and she asked Joe if they could go to a different restaurant, where she spent the evening telling him—yet again—about the failings of her boss.

Later, Amanda recognized that she had been going around in circles and had achieved nothing except to ruin her evening and Joe's too.

After Amanda had practiced mindfulness for a while, the same scenario occurred again. This time she took a step back, by getting in touch with her breathing, to consider her choices. In the end, she stayed and had her dinner while conversing about matters of mutual interest to herself and Joe. She still wasn't glad her boss was present, but she had a better evening than if she had reacted without considering her alternatives.

10. TEN WAYS TO REFOCUS

Mindfulness involves returning to awareness of what is happening in the activities of your daily life and doing so without judgment or comment, at least for some moments. To refocus on the go try these ten ideas:

1. **Tune in to the sounds and activities around you without passing judgment for a few moments at least.** For instance, pause and notice voices, footsteps, a radio in the distance, the sound of cars passing by.

2. **Choose a color and decide to notice that color as you go about your day.** You will begin to notice not only objects, but people who would otherwise have passed by in a haze of unawareness.

3. **Now and then, check if you need to straighten or relax your back a little.** Many of us fall into a sort of slump or slouch if we're sitting at a desk or watching TV. That's why noticing your back is a good awareness exercise.

4. **Count backward from sixty as you watch the second hand go around.** If you don't have a watch or clock with a second hand, perhaps you can put a virtual watch with a second hand on your computer screen (they are widely available and free). As you look at the second hand going around, count down to zero and keep bringing your mind back to what you are doing.

5. **Check your breathing instead of your email.** One of the great distractions that takes us out of contact with ourselves and our reality is endless checking of Twitter, Facebook, email and other media. Try to do these at set times, instead of obsessively distracting yourself. If you feel the need to check something, check your breathing.

6. **Notice where your body is in contact with a surface.** This could be a chair, a desk, your keyboard, your phone, the bannister, an escalator

rail, the floor, the ground or bedclothes, to name a few. Awareness in everyday situations like these takes no time, but reduces levels of stress and general hassle.

7. **Check out the energy of other people.** As you look at other people you can usually see if they are slumped, energetic, bubbly, tense, joyful and so on. In traditional mindfulness practice, paying attention to others is seen as a means of taking excessive focus off yourself.

8. **Remember where you are.** The act of remembering that you are in the office, walking down the street, on the train, etc. brings you right out of the trance so many of us spend so much of our time in.

9. **Choose one of the senses (touch, taste, smell, sight, hearing) and become aware of what it brings you.** Perhaps for this exercise you might pick a sense that you usually neglect. For instance, you might notice the different smells in a supermarket, department store or on the street.

10. **Drink water mindfully.** Instead of glugging, try drinking your water mindfully, noticing what it tastes and feels like.

RESOURCES: WHERE TO FIND OUT MORE

ON THE WEB

Free Mindfulness: www.freemindfulness.org. This brings together many good, free resources, including audios (some by me).

Everyday Mindfulness: www.everyday-mindfulness.org. A very accessible website with articles, links and discussion forums.

Mindful: www.mindful.org. The website of *Mindful* magazine with lots of articles, interviews and tips.

Wildmind: www.wildmind.org. Articles (including some by me) and online courses on one of the longer-running, more user-friendly Buddhist/mindfulness websites. I have done some of their courses as a paying customer and I would recommend them.

ToDo Institute: www.todoinstitute.org. A long-running website bringing Japanese mindfulness to the West. It includes lots of free stuff and very accessible material. The institute offers monthlong online courses (as well as residential courses in Vermont). I have done some of these courses as a paying customer and would recommend them.

Breathworks: www.breathworks-mindfulness.org.uk. Primarily aimed at people who suffer from chronic illness, Breathworks is based on the experience of Vidyamala Burch, who came to mindfulness through living with chronic pain. Breathworks offers courses in various locations.

Mindfulness Matters: www.mindfulnessmatters.ie. Good ideas on mindfulness for children in the resources section. You can also get mindfulness CDs for children here.

Mindfulness in Schools: www.mindfulnessinschools.org. Lots of good information on applying mindfulness in education. The website will link you to research and is a valuable resource for anyone interested in this aspect of mindfulness.

Padraig O'Morain: www.padraigomorain.com. My website has lots of free resources, including audios, articles and sign-up pages for a free newsletter and a free daily mindfulness reminder.

POPULAR SMARTPHONE APPS

There weren't any smartphones for the first 2,495 or so years of mindfulness practice, but you can get good smartphone and tablet apps now, if you want to enlist technology to help with your practice. These are three of the most popular:

Insight Timer. As its name suggests, this free app is designed for timing your mindfulness meditations. It also tells you (visually) how many people are using the app at any one time and where in the world they are. It includes guided meditation and forums.

The Mindfulness App. An inexpensive, very popular and easy-to-use app. You can use guided or silent meditations or create your own mindfulness periods of one minute and up.

Headspace. Andy Puddicombe's app is stylish and popular. You get ten days of free meditation and pay for a subscription for all the features.

BOOKS

Wherever You Go, There You Are: Mindfulness Meditation for Everyday Life, **Jon Kabat-Zinn.** Short mindfulness reflections by Kabat-Zinn, whose work with chronic-pain patients at the hospital attached to the University of Massachusetts brought mindfulness into the mainstream. A book for dipping in to and well worth having on your shelf.

The Happiness Trap, **Russ Harris.** A clear and engaging book based on Acceptance and Commitment Therapy, which is a very accessible Australian take on mindfulness. The book is short and uses clear language and examples.

Mindfulness: A Practical Guide to Finding Peace in a Frantic World, **Mark Williams and Danny Penman.** A thorough guide to all aspects of mindfulness by two authors, one of whom, Professor Mark Williams, has done the key research on mindfulness and depression.

Sane New World: Taming the Mind, **Ruby Wax.** The mindfulness section of this bestselling book on the emotional journey of one of the world's best-known comedians is clear, witty and refreshingly free of bull.

Light Mind: Mindfulness for Daily Living, **Padraig O'Morain.** A guide to bringing mindfulness into your daily life.

How to Train a Wild Elephant & Other Adventures in Mindfulness, **Jan Chozen Bays.** A gem of a book with many simple mindfulness ideas and good, clear explanations of how they contribute to the general practice of mindfulness.

Mindfulness for Health: A Practical Guide to Relieving Pain, Reducing Stress and Restoring Wellbeing, **Vidyamala Burch and Danny Penman.** An excellent reference for anybody who is coping with chronic pain, but also a great guide to mindfulness in itself. Vidyamala Burch, who lives with chronic pain, writes from the perspective of one who has walked the walk.

The Mindful Way Through Depression: Freeing Yourself from Chronic Unhappiness, **Mark Williams, John Teasdale, Zindel Segal and Jon Kabat-Zinn.** The standard mindfulness guide—and deservedly so—for people suffering recurring bouts of depression. Useful and clearly written.

KEEPING IN TOUCH WITH ME

If, after reading this book and trying out the mindfulness practices described here, you'd like to continue to get mindfulness ideas and resources from me, here are some of the many ways you can do that:

- **Mindfulness newsletter:** Thousands of subscribers to this free newsletter get new mindfulness ideas, quotes, links to resources and information on my courses by email. Sign up through my website at www.padraigomorain.com.

- **The Daily Bell:** This daily email contains a single quote or idea, usually sent out as soon as I get to my desk (and after my first coffee) in the morning. It's free and you can sign up at www.padraigomorain.com.

- **Courses:** My one-day and three-day courses take place mostly in the Republic of Ireland and in Northern Ireland. Courses in Great Britain and elsewhere will be announced in the newsletter and on www.padraigomorain.com.

- **Twitter:** Follow me on Twitter for mindfulness ideas, quotes and links. My Twitter handle is @PadraigOMorain.

- **Facebook:** My Facebook mindfulness page is www.facebook.com/PadraigOMorainMindfulness.

- **Blog:** My mindfulness blog is at www.lightmindblog.blogspot.com.

- **Website:** (the best place to start connecting with me) www.padraigomorain.com.

- **Email:** pomorain@gmx.com

ONE LAST THING . . .

YouTube has become a terrific resource for anyone interested in mindfulness. Search there for videos with Mark Williams (Oxford University), Vidyamala Burch (Breathworks), Jon Kabat-Zinn (probably the major figure in modern mindfulness), Ruby Wax (the no-bull- . . . lady) and many others.

ACKNOWLEDGMENTS

I wish to acknowledge the influence of the work of the following people on my mindfulness practice and on aspects of this book: Jon Kabat-Zinn, Mark Williams, Nyanaponika Thera, David K. Reynolds, Gregg Krech and Linda Anderson Krech. Thanks to my agent, Susan Feldstein of the Feldstein Agency, and to Liz Gough, who oversaw the project, with dynamism and warmth, for Yellow Kite. Finally, my thanks to Marcella Finnerty, who told me, when I was searching for a topic, that if I wrote a mindfulness book aimed at busy people she would buy it and all her friends would too.

INDEX

ABOUT THE AUTHOR

Padraig O'Morain is a writer and psychotherapist. He has practiced mindfulness for a quarter of a century. During that time, he has trained a wide variety of people in mindfulness—from accountants to search-and-rescue crews—in both Ireland and the UK. He writes a weekly column for *The Irish Times* and his books include *Light Mind—Mindfulness for Daily Living* and a poetry collection, *The Blue Guitar*. He lives in Dublin with his wife and two daughters.